AF448747

BLAKE RADCLIFFE

WARRIOR MINDSET 2.0

THE NEXT LEVEL OF RESILIENCE AND PERFORMANCE

Disclaimer

The content of this book is provided for informational purposes only and is not intended as medical advice, nor should it be used to diagnose, treat, cure, or prevent any physical or mental health condition. This book does not serve as a substitute for professional medical advice, examination, diagnosis, or treatment. Always seek the advice of your physician or other qualified health provider with any questions you may have regarding a medical condition. Never disregard professional medical advice or delay in seeking it because of something you have read in this book. By using the information provided in this book, the reader agrees to assume full responsibility and risk associated with their use, and releases the author from any liability for any direct or indirect damages or losses resulting from the use of such information.

Table of Contents

Dedicated to my brother,

Michael Radcliffe,

whose strength and resilience

continue to inspire me every day

Introduction

Foreword

In today's ever-changing world, the need for mental resilience and peak performance has never been more critical. As we navigate the complexities of modern life, from economic uncertainties to the relentless flow of information, it becomes essential to develop a mindset that can withstand and thrive in the face of adversity. This is the foundation of "Warrior Mindset 2.0."

Over the past twenty years, I have had the opportunity to work with remarkable individuals and teams across various fields. From consulting with military units and government agencies to coaching elite athletes and corporate executives, I have dedicated my career to understanding and teaching the principles that support cognitive elasticity and optimal performance. This is a comprehensive guide that integrates the latest research in neuroscience, positive psychology, and emerging technologies. What makes this approach distinct is its emphasis on not only the physical and psychological aspects of elasticity but also the emotional and psychological components. This perspective is crucial for addressing the multifaceted challenges we face today. One of the most significant influences on my work has been a deeply personal experience. Early in my consulting career, my younger brother Michael, who has always been my best friend and a source of inspiration, was involved in a severe car accident that left him paralyzed from the waist down. This tragedy tested my strength in ways I had never imagined. It forced me to apply my teachings on a very personal level and deepened my understanding of true cognitive toughness. Michael's determination and strength in the face of such adversity have profoundly influenced my approach to resilience and performance. His journey and unwavering spirit are at the heart of the principles I share in this book. Through his example, I have learned that this is not just about enduring difficulties but also about embracing the growth that comes from them. The book is the result of years of research, personal experience, and professional practice. It offers practical strategies for tackling modern challenges and achieving optimal performance in every aspect of life. Whether you are striving for excellence in your profession, leading a team through complex situations, or seeking to build endurance in your personal life, I hope this book provides you with valuable insights and tools.

In the past, the concept of adaptability and performance was relatively straightforward. We trained our bodies and minds to endure physical hardships and stressful situations, relying on time-tested procedures that had worked for generations. However, the landscape of our lives has dramatically changed, necessitating a profound upgrade in our approach to performance. Here's why: we live in a world where the pace of life is faster than ever before. Technology, while incredibly beneficial, has also introduced new challenges. We are constantly bombarded with information, much of it conflicting or overwhelming. This continuous influx of data can lead to decision fatigue, anxiety, and a feeling of being perpetually "on." Economic uncertainties, global political shifts, and the rapid pace of technological advancement mean that our personal and professional environments are in a state of constant flux. Conventional methods, which often focused on enduring and pushing through, are no longer sufficient. We need plans that help us adapt and thrive amid this complexity, not just survive it. One of the most significant changes in modern life is the blurring of boundaries between work and personal time. The advent of digital connectivity means that work can follow us home and personal issues can intrude on work time. This erosion of boundaries creates a unique set of stressors that previous generations did not face. These approaches often emphasized separation: work was left at the office, and home issues stayed at home. Today, we must develop ways that allow us to manage and integrate these overlapping aspects of our lives. This requires a more nuanced understanding of stress management and emotional regulation.

Another crucial factor necessitating an upgrade in our approach is the increased awareness of mental health issues. In the past, it was often stigmatized or ignored. Today, we recognize that it is as important as physical health, if not more so. Modern strategies must encompass systems for maintaining it, recognizing the signs of burnout, and seeking help when needed. This approach acknowledges that our minds and bodies are deeply interconnected, and optimal performance cannot be achieved without addressing both. Recent advancements in neuroscience and positive psychology have provided us with a deeper understanding of how our brains work and how we can harness this knowledge to improve hardiness and performance. We now know that this is not a fixed trait but a set of skills that can be developed and strengthened over time. Positive psychology emphasizes the importance of building on our strengths and fostering a growth mindset. These insights have led to the development of more effective means for enhancing cerebral toughness, such as mindfulness practices, cognitive-behavioral designs, and the cultivation of gratitude and optimism. These methods go beyond the traditional "grit and bear it" approach, offering a more sustainable path. The nature of stress has also evolved. While our ancestors faced physical threats that required immediate and intense bodily responses, modern stressors are often chronic and psychological. This shift means that our bodies are in a near-constant state of low-level stress, which can lead to a range of health issues, from anxiety and depression to cardiovascular disease. Accustomed courses, which often focus on short-term stress management, are not equipped to handle the long-term nature of modern stress. We need plans that promote recovery and regeneration, helping us to manage stress more effectively over the long haul. This includes practices like adequate sleep, regular physical activity, and modes for emotional regulation. In the modern world, emotional health is just as important as physical health. We face a barrage of emotional challenges daily, from interpersonal conflicts to the pressures of social media, as one of the most pervasive challenges of our time is the omnipresence of social media and digital distractions. Platforms designed to connect us often end up consuming significant portions of our attention, leading to fragmented focus and decreased productivity. This constant connectivity can also foster unrealistic comparisons and exacerbate feelings of inadequacy or anxiety. Long-established methods did not account for the relentless nature of these digital intrusions. Modern strategies must include methods for managing digital consumption and maintaining brain clarity amidst the noise. Systems such as digital detoxes, setting boundaries for technology use, and cultivating mindfulness are essential for maintaining focus and emotional well-being. By learning to navigate the digital landscape with intention and control, we can protect our health resources and enhance our overall performance. This aspect is crucial for anyone seeking to thrive in today's tech-centric world, where the ability to disconnect and recharge is just as important as staying informed and connected. Developing emotional adaptability means learning to manage our emotions effectively, maintain healthy relationships, and find meaning and purpose in our lives. Standard procedures often neglected the emotional component, focusing primarily on physical endurance and brain toughness. However, without it, it is impossible to achieve it. Modern ones must include styles for developing emotional intelligence, such as empathy, self-awareness, and effective communication. Finally, the rapid pace of change in the modern world means that continuous learning and adaptation are some of the most critical components. We must be willing to update our skills, learn new technologies, and adapt to new ways of working and living. Customary ones often emphasized static techniques that were effective for a particular set of circumstances. Today, we need a dynamic approach that allows us to remain flexible and adaptable in the face of ongoing change. This means embracing a growth mindset, seeking out new learning opportunities, and being open to change.

The traditional approaches, while valuable, are no longer sufficient to meet the demands of our modern world. We need enhanced ones that address the complexity of modern life, the erosion of boundaries between work and personal time, the importance of mental health, the insights from neuroscience and positive psychology, the long-term nature of modern stress, the necessity of emotional strength, and the importance of continuous learning and adaptation. My work is designed to provide these enhanced programs. It is a comprehensive guide that integrates the latest research with practical, actionable ones. By adopting these, we can not only survive the challenges of modern life but thrive and achieve our fullest potential. I invite you to join me on this journey. Embrace the challenges, apply the principles outlined in these pages, and discover the strength within you to achieve your fullest potential. Together, we can build a more resilient, focused, and high-performing self.

Blake Radcliffe

The Phone Call that Changed Everything

It was a typical Tuesday afternoon when I received the phone call that would change my life forever. I was in the middle of a consulting session with a high-profile client, discussing policies for enhancing team performance, when my phone buzzed insistently. Normally, I wouldn't have answered, but something told me to pick up. On the other end of the line was a voice I recognized immediately—it was my mother, and she was barely holding it together.

"Blake, it's Michael. There's been an accident. You need to come to the hospital."

In that instant, my world turned upside down. My younger brother Michael, my best friend and constant source of inspiration, had been in a severe car accident. As I drove to the hospital, my mind raced with a thousand thoughts and fears. I felt a profound sense of helplessness, a deep pit of dread forming in my stomach. When I arrived, the doctors informed me that Michael had suffered a spinal cord injury and was paralyzed from the waist down. The news hit me like a ton of bricks. I could barely process the information. Michael was an exceptional athlete, full of life and energy. The thought of him being confined to a wheelchair was unimaginable. My initial struggle was not just about coping with the reality of his condition but also dealing with the overwhelming emotions that came with it—fear, anger, guilt, and a profound sense of loss. In the immediate aftermath of the accident, I found myself relying on basic coping procedures. These included setting small, achievable goals for each day, seeking solace in routine tasks, and leaning on the initial shock to propel me into action mode. I tried to stay busy, focusing on practical tasks like arranging medical appointments and managing logistical details. However, many of these approaches were short-term fixes that only temporarily masked the underlying emotional turmoil. I quickly realized that I needed more sustainable approaches to manage the emotional and psychological toll of the situation. The days and weeks following the accident were some of the hardest of my life. I was torn between my professional obligations and the need to be there for my brother. Each day was a battle to maintain some semblance of normalcy while my heart was breaking. The emotional toll was immense. I struggled with feelings of guilt, questioning whether there was something I could have done to prevent the accident. Helplessness washed over me as I watched Michael grapple with his new reality. Throughout this period, the support of family, friends, and professional networks was invaluable. My parents were a constant source of strength, providing not only emotional support but also practical help with Michael's care. Friends rallied around us, offering their time and resources to ease our burden. Professionally, my colleagues and clients were understanding and supportive, giving me the space I needed to be with my brother. This network of support made a significant difference, helping us navigate the immediate crisis and providing a foundation upon which we could rebuild. It reinforced the idea that this is not just an individual trait but a communal one, reliant on strong, supportive relationships.

Michael, always the fighter, faced his new circumstances with a bravery that left me in awe. He refused to let his injury define him, displaying a strength and determination that was both humbling and inspiring. I spent countless hours at the hospital, helping him through physical therapy sessions, learning how to assist him with daily tasks, and providing emotional support. We shared many difficult conversations, tears, and moments of frustration, but through it all, Michael's spirit remained unbroken. His toughness in the face of such a life-altering event became a beacon of hope for me. Balancing my professional responsibilities with the need to support my brother was one of the most challenging aspects of this period. On one hand, I had ongoing commitments to clients and projects that required my attention and expertise. On the other hand, my heart and mind were constantly with Michael, and I wanted to be by his side as much as possible. There were days when I felt pulled in multiple directions, struggling to give my best in both realms. This tension forced me to reevaluate my priorities and find new ways to manage my time and energy. It became clear that traditional techniques, which often emphasize pushing through and enduring, were insufficient. I needed a more balanced approach that allowed me to be effective at work while also being fully present for my brother.

It was during these challenging times that the concept of "Warrior Mindset 2.0" began to take shape, but it didn't happen immediately. The first few weeks were solely focused on Michael and helping him adjust to his new life. The idea of creating a new approach came later, as I reflected on the incredible strength Michael demonstrated. I realized that the planning I had been teaching needed to evolve to encompass not just physical and cerebral endurance but also the deep emotional and psychological resilience that Michael embodied. The accident and its aftermath led to a profound evolution in my professional philosophy regarding intellectual balance and performance. Previously, my work focused heavily on physical and rational endurance, drawing from my experiences with elite athletes and military personnel. However, watching Michael's journey highlighted the importance of emotional healthiness and the need to address the psychological aspects of facing adversity. This shift in perspective influenced my consulting and coaching approaches. I began to incorporate more methods that addressed the full spectrum of human experience—physical and emotional. This integrated approach became a cornerstone of the project, emphasizing the interconnectedness of all its aspects. This book is about integrating the latest research in neuroscience, positive psychology, and emerging technologies to build comprehensive strategies to go down a healthier route. It's about embracing vulnerability, fostering a growth mindset, and developing ways that can help us navigate the unique challenges of the digital age. The need for an upgraded approach is clear. Today, we face an array of challenges that our predecessors could never have imagined. From the constant connectivity of the digital world to the economic uncertainties and global crises, the stressors we face are more pervasive and persistent. Research has shown that the nature of stress has evolved. While our ancestors faced immediate physical threats, modern stressors are often chronic and psychological. This shift requires a new set of tools that can help us manage long-term stress and prevent burnout. For example, studies in neuroscience have highlighted the importance of neuroplasticity—the brain's ability to adapt and change in response to experiences. Positive psychology also plays a crucial role in this new approach. Practices such as gratitude, optimism, and the cultivation of positive relationships are integral to maintaining your emotional well-being and enhancing performance. Developing the book was a journey that required me to reevaluate everything I thought I knew about adaptability and performance. I had to dig deep into my own experiences, both personal and professional, to find new schemes that could address the unique challenges of modern life. Michael's journey was a constant source of inspiration. His determination to adapt to his new reality and his unwavering spirit taught me more about emotional balance than any textbook ever could. I began to incorporate courses that went beyond old-established training. Mindfulness and meditation became central components of my daily routine, helping me manage stress and maintain focus. I also started to emphasize the importance of recovery and regeneration, recognizing that this is not just about pushing through but also about knowing when to rest and recharge. One of the key elements of it is the integration of emotional security. This involves not only managing our own emotions but also developing empathy and strong interpersonal relationships. Emotional intelligence is a critical component of brain toughness, and it requires continuous practice and development.

The latest research in neuroscience and psychology has provided invaluable insights: recent studies have shown that our mental and emotional states are profoundly influenced by various factors that we can learn to manage and optimize. For instance, the field of positive psychology has demonstrated the powerful effects of cultivating positive emotions and strengths-based approaches. Practices such as gratitude journaling, which involves regularly writing about things you are thankful for, have been shown to improve mood and overall well-being. Additionally, cognitive-behavioral strategies, which help reframe negative thought patterns, are crucial for developing a resilient mindset. Research on stress management has revealed that meditation can significantly reduce stress levels, improve concentration, and enhance emotional regulation. These findings underscore the importance of incorporating awareness practices into daily routines. Studies have also highlighted the critical role of social support networks: building strong, supportive relationships can provide emotional sustenance and practical help during challenging times, which is a key component of the project. The understanding of chronic stress and its impact on the body and mind has led to the development of more effective stress management modes. The book is designed to offer readers practical approaches for tackling modern challenges and achieving optimal performance in every aspect of life. My vision for this book is to provide a comprehensive toolkit that integrates the latest research with actionable insights. Readers can expect to find practical exercises, real-life examples, and evidence-based systems that address the complexities of contemporary life. Whether you are striving for excellence in your profession, leading a team through difficult times, or seeking to build personal balance, this book aims to equip you with the tools you need to succeed. The principles outlined here are not just theoretical concepts; they are tried and tested methods that have helped me and countless others navigate the challenges of modern life.

As we move forward, it is essential to continuously adapt and refine our plans. The challenges we face will continue to evolve, and so must our approaches to overcoming them. Our world is marked by rapid changes in technology, fluctuating economic landscapes, and increasing social complexities. Each new development presents unique obstacles and opportunities, requiring us to stay agile and proactive. Our understanding of human performance is constantly expanding. Advances in neuroscience, psychology, and behavioral science provide us with deeper insights into how we can enhance our mental and emotional strength. These insights allow us to develop more effective procedures for managing stress, staying focused, and maintaining peak performance even in the face of adversity. However, it is important to remember that this is not a static trait; it is a dynamic process that requires ongoing effort and adaptation. In the chapters that follow, we will explore the principles that form the foundation of a modern, comprehensive approach. Whether you are an athlete, a business leader, or someone looking to improve yourself, these tools are designed to help you navigate the complexities of modern life with greater confidence and competence. You will learn about techniques for managing stress, which can help you stay calm and focused under pressure. We will discuss the importance of emotional resilience and how to cultivate it through practices like gratitude, optimism, and building strong support networks. Additionally, we will delve into programs for maintaining motivation and focus, which are crucial for achieving long-term goals and sustaining high performance. This journey is about more than just enduring hardships; it is about thriving and growing through them. By adopting a new, personal approach, we can better equip ourselves to handle whatever challenges come our way. The goal is to build a toolkit that you can draw upon in any situation, helping you to remain adaptable, resilient, and high-performing. I encourage you to stay open-minded and committed to continuous improvement. Adaptability is a skill that can be developed and strengthened over time, and the effort you put into cultivating it will pay off in countless ways. Let's move forward with the confidence that we have the tools and knowledge to not only face the challenges ahead but to excel in overcoming them.

Michael's journey directly influenced the development of my work: reflecting on this journey, I am profoundly grateful for Michael and the lessons he has taught me. His strength has not only inspired this book but have also shaped the way I view the world. Our relationship has deepened through this shared experience, and I am proud to say that Michael continues to thrive despite his challenges. It has been several years since the accident, and while there have been many hurdles, Michael has faced each one with an unshakable force. He has become an advocate for others facing similar challenges, and his story continues to inspire everyone who hears it. His unwavering spirit and determination to adapt to his new reality served as a constant source of inspiration. I observed how he faced each challenge head-on, refusing to let his circumstances define him. This observation led me to integrate methods that focus on emotional and psychological strength, alongside more fixed methods. Michael's experiences underscored the importance of adaptability, empathy, and the ability to find meaning in adversity. His story became a central narrative in the development of this new approach, illustrating the power of the human spirit and the potential for growth even in the face of seemingly insurmountable obstacles. His infinite wisdom has not only inspired this book but have also shaped the way I view the world. Our relationship has deepened through this shared experience, and I am proud to say that Michael continues to thrive despite his challenges. It has been several years since the accident, and while there have been many hurdles, Michael has faced each one with an unwavering spirit. He has become an advocate for others facing similar challenges, and his story continues to inspire everyone who hears it. "Warrior Mindset 2.0" is as much Michael's story as it is mine. His journey is woven throughout these pages. I hope that through this book, you too can find the inspiration to overcome your challenges and achieve your fullest potential.

Part I: Foundations of the Modern Warrior Mindset

New Frontiers of Mental Toughness

In today's world, challenges come at us faster than we can dodge them. Economic uncertainty and information overload are two of the biggest contenders in the ring, each packing a powerful punch. First up, let's talk about economic uncertainty. Gone are the days when job security meant a gold watch after 40 years of service. Now, we live in an era where entire industries can crumble overnight, where gig work is becoming the norm, and where financial stability feels more like a mirage than a milestone. The global economy is a roller coaster ride, and not the fun kind with cotton candy at the end. It's more like the one where the safety harness feels a bit too loose, and you're not entirely sure you'll make it back in one piece. Consider the 2008 financial crisis, a stark reminder of how quickly things can go south. Millions lost their jobs, homes, and savings. Fast forward to the COVID-19 pandemic, which brought the world to its knees once again, disrupting economies and livelihoods on a scale we hadn't seen in decades. This constant state of flux means that adaptability isn't just a desirable trait—it's essential. Navigating this landscape requires a brain toughness that can withstand the ups and downs, that can take a hit and come back swinging. Economic uncertainty isn't just a distant threat; it's a persistent undercurrent that influences our daily lives. Let's delve deeper into how this uncertainty manifests and affects our mental health. Consider the gig economy, which has grown exponentially over the past decade. On one hand, it offers flexibility and autonomy; on the other, it brings instability and a lack of traditional benefits like health insurance and retirement plans. This shift means that workers must constantly hustle to secure their next gig, creating a backdrop of perpetual stress and uncertainty. Navigating this landscape requires not only adaptability but also a proactive approach to financial planning and self-care. Another facet of economic uncertainty is the rapid pace of technological advancement. Automation and artificial intelligence are reshaping industries, rendering some jobs obsolete while creating new ones. This evolution demands a continuous commitment to learning and skill development. The modern worker must be a lifelong learner, willing to pivot and adapt as the job market evolves. Embracing a growth mindset, as Carol Dweck describes, is crucial for maintaining brain toughness in this ever-changing environment. We can also see the impact of economic uncertainty on our well-being. Financial instability can lead to chronic stress, which is linked to a range of health issues, from anxiety and depression to cardiovascular diseases. Developing strength involves not only managing external circumstances but also cultivating inner strength. Practices like stress management techniques become essential tools for maintaining emotional and physical well-being. Let's not overlook the social implications of economic uncertainty. Inequality and lack of access to opportunities can create a sense of hopelessness. Building community support systems and advocating for equitable policies are ways we can collectively address these challenges. A resilient mindset recognizes the importance of both individual and collective actions in creating a more stable and just society.

Now, let's switch gears to information overload. In the age of the internet, we are bombarded with more information than our ancestors encountered in a lifetime. Every day, we're swamped with emails, notifications, news updates, social media feeds, and the endless scroll of content vying for our attention. It's like drinking from a fire hose, and it's no wonder our brains are struggling to keep up.

The sheer volume of information is staggering. According to a study by IBM, we create 2.5 quintillion bytes of data each day. That's a mind-boggling number, and it's growing exponentially. Our brains, however, haven't evolved at the same pace. We're still wired to process information in a way that was suited for survival in the wild, not for sifting through gigabytes of data. This overload not only hampers our ability to focus but also increases stress and anxiety levels. Let's take a closer look at the impact of this constant influx of information. Decision fatigue is a real phenomenon; the more decisions we make throughout the day, the more our cognitive resources are depleted. By the time we're faced with a critical choice, we might be running on empty, leading to poor judgment and mistakes. The quality of information varies wildly, and separating the signal from the noise becomes an exhausting task. In a world where misinformation can spread like wildfire, staying informed yet discerning is a herculean challenge. One of the most insidious effects of information overload is the erosion of our attention span. Research by Microsoft suggests that the average human attention span has dropped to eight seconds, shorter than that of a goldfish. This decline makes it difficult to engage in deep, focused work, which is essential for complex problem-solving and creative endeavors. Overcoming this challenge requires deliberate practices to enhance our attention span, such as setting aside time for distraction-free work and training our minds through meditation. Another critical aspect is the impact on our memory and learning processes. The constant influx of information can lead to cognitive overload, where our brains struggle to process and retain new information. This can result in superficial understanding and hinder long-term knowledge retention. To combat this, we need to adopt effective learning strategies, such as spaced repetition and active recall, which enhance memory consolidation and deepen our understanding. Moreover, the nature of online interactions contributes to mental fatigue. Social media platforms, with their emphasis on instant gratification and superficial engagement, can leave us feeling disconnected and dissatisfied. Studies have shown that excessive social media use is linked to increased feelings of loneliness and depression. Developing a balanced approach to technology use, where we prioritize meaningful connections over passive consumption, is vital for our well-being. Let's also consider the role of digital minimalism, a concept popularized by Cal Newport. Digital minimalism advocates for a focused and intentional use of technology, where we carefully curate our digital environments to support our values and goals. By reducing unnecessary digital clutter, we can create space for activities that truly matter, such as face-to-face interactions, creative pursuits, and physical exercise. The challenge of information overload extends beyond personal well-being to societal implications. The spread of misinformation and the polarization of public discourse are direct consequences of unchecked information proliferation. Developing critical thinking skills and media literacy becomes essential for navigating this complex landscape. We must learn to question sources, verify facts, and engage in constructive dialogues to foster a more informed and cohesive society. Lastly, let's touch on the importance of creating rational space for reflection and creativity. In a world that constantly demands our attention, setting aside time for solitude and contemplation can be a powerful antidote. Practices such as journaling, nature walks, and meditation allow us to disconnect from the noise and reconnect with our inner selves. These moments of quiet reflection are not only restorative but also crucial for fostering creativity and innovation. By deepening our understanding of these contemporary challenges and implementing strategies to manage their impact, we can cultivate a modern warrior mindset that is resilient, adaptable, and equipped to thrive in an uncertain world. But there's more to this story. The nature of the information we consume also plays a crucial role. Negative news tends to dominate the headlines because it captures our attention more effectively than positive stories. This constant exposure to negativity can skew our perception of the world, making us feel more anxious and less secure. The psychological toll of this negativity bias is significant, contributing to feelings of helplessness and despair. To top it off, social media platforms are designed to keep us hooked, using algorithms that prioritize engagement over well-being. The endless scroll, the likes, the shares—it's all part of a meticulously crafted system to capture our attention and keep us coming back for more. This can lead to a vicious cycle of distraction, where our attention is constantly pulled in different directions, leaving little room for deep, focused work. So, how do we navigate these contemporary challenges? It starts with acknowledging their existence and understanding their impact. Recognizing that economic uncertainty is a constant in today's world helps us prepare mentally for the ups and downs. Building a financial safety net, diversifying income streams, and staying adaptable in our careers are practical steps we can take to mitigate the impact of economic shocks. When it comes to information overload, we need to be proactive in managing our cerebral bandwidth. This might mean setting boundaries for technology use, curating our information sources, and practicing digital detoxes to give our brains a break. Developing habits that promote deep work and focus, such as time-blocking and mindfulness, can help us reclaim our cognitive resources and improve our decision-making abilities. In the face of these formidable challenges, the modern warrior mindset is not about denying the existence of difficulties but about facing them head-on with adaptability. It's about understanding that brain toughness isn't just about enduring hardships but about thriving amidst them. By recognizing the forces at play and taking strategic steps to counteract their effects, we can build a mind fortress capable of withstanding the storms of the modern world.

Modern brain toughness isn't about gritting your teeth and pushing through at any cost. It's about maintaining a positive outlook even in the face of adversity. Let's explore what this looks like with some examples and narratives that illustrate these concepts in action.

Consider **Jane**, a startup founder navigating the turbulent waters of the tech industry. Jane's journey is a testament to modern brain toughness. After years of developing her app, she finally launched it, only to be met with lukewarm reception. Users found the interface confusing, and critics were quick to pounce. Rather than seeing this as a failure, Jane viewed it as a learning opportunity. She dove into user feedback, embracing the criticism instead of shying away from it. This approach required a thick skin and a willingness to confront uncomfortable truths. Jane's toughness was evident in her ability to stay focused on her vision while adapting her strategy. She revamped the app, incorporating user suggestions and re-launched it with a more intuitive design. Her persistence paid off. The app began to gain traction, and within a year, it had a robust user base and positive reviews. It is not just about enduring hardships but also about learning from them and evolving. It's about maintaining a growth mindset, where challenges are seen as opportunities for development rather than insurmountable obstacles.

Let's take a look at **Tom**, an emergency room nurse who exemplifies modern cerebral toughness in a high-stress environment. The emergency room is a place where life-and-death decisions are made daily, and the pressure can be overwhelming. Tom's ability to stay calm and composed under pressure is a crucial aspect of his toughness. One night, the ER was flooded with patients following a multi-car accident. Amidst the chaos, Tom noticed a child who had been overlooked in the triage process. Despite the frantic environment, he maintained his composure and quickly assessed the child's condition, prioritizing her care. His quick thinking and calm demeanor under pressure not only saved the child's life but also helped manage the overall situation more effectively. Tom is characterized by his ability to stay focused and perform optimally under stress. He practices mindfulness and stress management techniques regularly, which help him maintain his calm in high-pressure situations. This example illustrates that modern toughness involves proactive self-care and the development of skills that enable one to handle stress effectively.

Next, consider **Mia**, a young athlete training for the Olympics. Mia's journey is fraught with physical and cerebral challenges, from grueling training sessions to the pressure of competition. Her toughness shines through her unwavering dedication and her ability to bounce back from setbacks. During a critical qualifying event, Mia suffered a severe injury that could have ended her career. Instead of succumbing to despair, she focused on her recovery with the same intensity she brought to her training. She worked closely with her physiotherapist, adhered strictly to her rehabilitation plan, and gradually regained her strength. Throughout this process, Mia kept a positive attitude, visualizing her return to competition. Mia's story underscores the role of optimism and perseverance in modern toughness. It's about maintaining hope and determination even when the odds are stacked against you. Her ability to recover from injury and return to peak performance illustrates the toughness that defines a modern warrior.

In the corporate world, **Sarah**, a tech employee, faced a company-wide layoff that left her uncertain about her future. Rather than spiraling into panic, Sarah took a proactive approach. She immediately updated her resume, reached out to her professional network, and began applying for new opportunities. Simultaneously, she enrolled in online courses to enhance her skills and make herself more marketable. Sarah's toughness was evident in her proactive response to the crisis. She didn't wait passively for her fate to be decided; she took control of her situation. This narrative highlights the importance of taking initiative and staying proactive in the face of uncertainty. Modern toughness involves not just enduring difficult times but actively seeking ways to improve and move forward.

Lastly, let's explore the story of **Raj**, a community leader who faced significant adversity in the wake of a natural disaster. When a devastating flood hit his town, Raj's home was destroyed, and his community was left in shambles. Despite his personal loss, Raj stepped up to lead the recovery efforts. He organized volunteers, coordinated with relief agencies, and provided support to those who had lost everything. Raj's toughness was evident in his selflessness and his ability to inspire others. Even when he was exhausted and overwhelmed, he remained a pillar of strength for his community. Raj's story illustrates that modern toughness is also about community leadership and support. It's about using one's strength to lift others and working together to overcome collective challenges.

From these examples and narratives, several key traits of modern toughness emerge. Each trait plays a crucial role in helping individuals navigate the complexities and adversities of today's world. Let's delve deeper into these traits to understand how they contribute to toughness. **Resilience** is the cornerstone of toughness. It's the capacity to recover quickly from difficulties and setbacks. It isn't about never failing; it's about bouncing back each time you do. Jane's journey with her startup illustrates this beautifully. Despite initial failure, she used the feedback to improve her app, showing that the focus involves learning and growing from experiences rather than being defeated by them. For athletes like Mia, it is a daily practice. Injury and disappointment are part of the sporting world, but it's the ability to recover and come back stronger that sets apart those who succeed. Developing it involves building a mindset that views challenges as opportunities for growth, and this can be cultivated through practices such as reflective journaling and goal setting. **Adaptability** is about being flexible and open to change. In our stressful society, rigid thinking can be a significant drawback. Adaptability means being able to pivot when circumstances change, whether it's a shift in the job market, new technology, or unexpected life events. Jane's ability to revamp her app based on user feedback and Tom's calm response to emergencies in the ER are perfect examples of adaptability. They demonstrate the importance of being able to think on your feet and adjust your strategies as needed. Cultivating adaptability involves embracing lifelong learning, being open to new experiences, and developing problem-solving skills that allow you to navigate new terrain effectively. **Optimism** is not about ignoring reality or being blindly positive. It's about maintaining hope and seeing possibilities even in difficult situations. Optimism fuels perseverance and is a powerful motivator in the face of adversity. Mia's determination to recover from her injury and Raj's leadership during the flood highlight how optimism can drive action and inspire others. Optimism can be cultivated through positive thinking exercises, gratitude practices, and by surrounding oneself with supportive and encouraging people. It's about training your mind to focus on what can be done, rather than what can't, and finding silver linings even in the darkest clouds. **Proactivity** is the trait of taking charge of situations rather than reacting passively to them. It's about being forward-thinking and anticipating challenges before they arise. Sarah's immediate actions after learning about the layoffs are a testament to the power of proactivity. She didn't wait for circumstances to dictate her future; she took the reins and created her own opportunities. Proactivity involves setting clear goals, planning ahead, and taking decisive action. It's about being a self-starter and continually seeking ways to improve and prepare for potential challenges. This trait can be enhanced by developing strong organizational skills, staying informed about trends and changes in your field, and consistently working on personal and professional development. Finally, **community support** is an often-overlooked aspect of rational elasticity. Raj's leadership in the aftermath of the flood demonstrates how supporting and leading others can fortify our ourselves. This is not solely an individual endeavor; it's about fostering connections and building a support network that can provide strength and encouragement during tough times. Community support involves active participation in social groups, being willing to help others, and seeking help when needed. It's about recognizing that collective strength can amplify individual strength. Building community support can be achieved through volunteering, joining professional or interest-based groups, and nurturing relationships with family, friends, and colleagues.

Developing the key traits of modern brain elasticity requires intentional effort and practice. Here are some practical steps to help cultivate each trait: by writing about your experiences and the lessons learned from them, you can gain valuable insights and develop a deeper understanding of how to navigate future challenges. Additionally, engaging in activities that push you out of your comfort zone can enhance your coping skills. Whether it's taking on a new physical challenge, learning a difficult skill, or tackling a complex problem, these experiences can strengthen your ability to adapt and thrive under pressure. **Adaptability** involves being flexible and open to change, which nowadays is crucial. Embracing lifelong learning is a key strategy for fostering adaptability. Continuously seeking new knowledge and skills keeps you prepared for shifts in your career or personal life. Taking on new projects or hobbies that require you to develop new skills and perspectives can also enhance your adaptability. For example, learning a new language or trying out a different style of cooking can broaden your horizons and make you more comfortable with change. **Optimism** helps maintain a positive outlook even in challenging times. Starting a gratitude journal is a simple yet powerful way to cultivate optimism. Each day, write down three things you're grateful for, no matter how small. This practice can shift your focus from what's going wrong to what's going right in your life. Additionally, practice reframing negative thoughts into positive ones. When faced with a difficult situation, consciously look for the silver lining or the lesson that can be learned. This shift in perspective can significantly impact your overall mindset. **Proactivity** means taking charge of situations rather than reacting passively. Setting SMART goals—goals that are Specific, Measurable, Achievable, Relevant, and Time-bound—is a practical approach to being proactive. Break your goals into actionable steps and regularly review your progress. This method helps you stay focused and motivated, ensuring that you're consistently working towards your objectives. Proactivity also involves anticipating potential challenges and preparing for them in advance, which can reduce stress and increase your effectiveness in achieving your goals. **Community Support** is about recognizing the importance of building strong connections with others. Volunteering for causes you care about can provide a sense of purpose and fulfillment; while also helping you connect with like-minded individuals. Joining a support group or a community club can offer a valuable network of people who can provide encouragement and assistance when needed. Making time to connect with loved ones and building meaningful relationships is crucial for your emotional well-being. These connections can offer support during tough times and contribute to your overall brain elasticity. By integrating these practical steps into your daily life, you can develop the key traits of modern perseverance. These traits—

adaptability, optimism, proactivity, and community support—are not just abstract concepts but actionable qualities that can be nurtured through consistent effort and practice. As you strengthen these traits, you'll find yourself better equipped to handle the complexities and adversities of today's world, emerging stronger and more resilient with each challenge you face.

To deepen our understanding of modern mental fortitude, we can draw valuable insights from influential works like "**Peak Performance**" by **Brad Stulberg and Steve Magness**, and "**Range**" by **David Epstein**. These books provide a wealth of knowledge on optimizing performance, cultivating it, and leveraging a broad skill set to navigate the complexities of today's world. "Peak Performance" emphasizes the delicate balance between stress and recovery as the foundation for achieving high performance. Stulberg and Magness argue that stress, when managed correctly, can be a powerful catalyst for growth. However, this stress must be counterbalanced with adequate recovery to prevent burnout. One of the key concepts from "Peak Performance" is the idea of periodization, which is commonly used in athletic training but can be applied to any area of life. Periodization involves cycling through phases of intense effort followed by periods of rest and recovery. This approach helps by ensuring that the body and mind are given time to recuperate and grow stronger. For example, Jane, our startup founder, used the concept of periodization by working intensely on her app's development and then taking deliberate breaks to recharge. By alternating between high-stress periods and recovery phases, she maintained her psychical and physical well-being, allowing her to persist through the challenges of launching a successful product. Another crucial idea from "Peak Performance" is the importance of intentional rest. Stulberg and Magness highlight that rest is not merely the absence of work but an active process that involves activities like sleep, appreciation, and hobbies that rejuvenate the mind and body. Tom, the emergency room nurse, practices meditation and stress management techniques to stay calm under pressure, demonstrating the value of intentional rest in maintaining high performance in a demanding job. David Epstein's "Range" challenges the traditional notion that early specialization is the key to success. Instead, Epstein argues that a wide range of experiences and skills can lead to greater creativity, problem-solving abilities, and adaptability. This concept is particularly relevant in today's rapidly changing world, where the ability to draw on diverse knowledge and experiences is invaluable. Epstein introduces the concept of the "kind" and "wicked" learning environments. In "kind" environments, patterns repeat, and feedback is immediate and accurate, making specialization effective. In contrast, "wicked" environments are unpredictable, with delayed and often inaccurate feedback, where broader skills and adaptable thinking are more advantageous. For example, Sarah, the tech employee, benefited from a broad skill set when faced with a layoff. Her diverse experiences and continuous learning allowed her to pivot quickly and find new opportunities. This adaptability is a core aspect of modern perseverance, as it enables individuals to navigate unexpected challenges with confidence and creativity. Epstein also highlights the importance of "match quality," which refers to the alignment between an individual's abilities and interests with the demands of their environment. Finding and pursuing roles that offer high match quality can lead to greater job satisfaction and performance. Mia, the young athlete, illustrates this concept by dedicating herself to a sport she is passionate about, which fuels her determination to overcome setbacks. Developing tenacity is essential for both personal and professional success. By integrating key principles such as balancing stress and recovery, embracing diverse experiences, pursuing match quality, and practicing intentional rest, we can build a resilient and adaptable mindset. Balancing stress and recovery is a fundamental aspect of modern determination. By incorporating regular breaks into our work schedules and prioritizing activities that promote relaxation and recovery—such as sleep, meditation, and hobbies—we can prevent burnout and enhance long-term stability. This balance ensures that we maintain our energy and focus, allowing us to handle challenges with a refreshed and resilient mindset. Embracing diverse experiences is another crucial element. Cultivating a broad range of skills and experiences enhances our adaptability and problem-solving abilities. This diversification not only makes us more adaptable but also fosters creativity and innovation by exposing us to new ways of thinking. The more varied our experiences, the better equipped we are to approach problems from multiple angles, enhancing our overall willpower. Pursuing match quality involves seeking roles and opportunities that align with our abilities and interests. This alignment boosts motivation, satisfaction, and performance, contributing significantly to it.

Reflecting on our strengths and passions, and seeking ways to integrate them into our career and personal life, can help us find this alignment. When our work resonates with our core interests and abilities, it becomes a source of energy rather than a drain, enhancing our overall effectiveness. Finding this alignment often involves introspection and experimentation, allowing us to discover what truly fulfills and motivates us. Intentional rest is an active and critical component of high performance. Rest is not merely the absence of work; it is a rejuvenating process that prepares us for future challenges. By integrating these principles into our approach to endurance, we can build a resilient, adaptable, and high-performing mindset. These strategies provide a solid foundation for navigating the uncertainties and challenges of the modern world, empowering us to thrive in both personal and professional endeavors. Developing modern endurance involves more than understanding key principles; it requires practical application in our daily lives. By establishing boundaries, diversifying our learning, reflecting on our interests, practicing mindfulness, and prioritizing sleep, we can enhance our adaptability to thrive in a complex world. Setting clear boundaries between work and rest is crucial for maintaining psychical and physical health. Designating specific times for work and leisure helps create a balanced lifestyle. For instance, allocate time slots during your day solely for work tasks, and stick to these without letting personal matters interfere. Similarly, set aside time for relaxation and personal activities, ensuring you honor this commitment to rest and recovery. This separation helps prevent burnout by ensuring that you get adequate rest, thus maintaining your energy levels and productivity. Establishing a boundary such as not checking work emails after a certain hour can significantly enhance your well-being. Engaging in learning activities outside your primary field can greatly enhance your adaptability and creativity. This involves taking online courses, reading books on various subjects, or participating in workshops and seminars. For example, a software engineer might benefit from learning about psychology or a business executive could gain insights from studying art. These activities broaden your perspective and equip you with a versatile skill set, making you more adaptable to change and better at problem-solving. The cross-pollination of ideas from different fields can spur innovative thinking and creative solutions, crucial components of tenacity. Regular reflection on your career and personal pursuits ensures alignment with your strengths and interests, which is essential for sustained motivation and satisfaction. Periodically assess your current roles and responsibilities to determine if they leverage your natural talents and passions. If there is a mismatch, consider making adjustments that bring you closer to roles offering higher match quality. This might involve seeking new opportunities within your current organization, pursuing further education or training, or even changing career paths. Aligning your activities with your core interests makes your work more fulfilling and energizing, thus enhancing your effectiveness. A consistent sleep routine is fundamental to psychical and physical well-being. Developing habits that promote good sleep hygiene can drastically improve your overall health and performance. This might involve reducing screen time before bed to minimize blue light exposure, keeping your bedroom dark and cool to create a sleep-friendly environment, and establishing a regular sleep schedule by going to bed and waking up at the same time each day. Quality sleep is essential for cognitive function, emotional stability, and physical health. Ensuring you are well-rested prepares you to tackle daily challenges with a clear and focused mind, thereby enhancing your willpower.

Principles of the Warrior Mindset

The warrior mindset has long been celebrated as a powerful and essential quality, transcending cultures and epochs. At its core, this mindset embodies discipline, honor, and an unwavering commitment to overcome adversity. It's a concept rooted deeply in history, yet it remains profoundly relevant today. Historically, this mindset was cultivated by ancient fighters like the Spartans, Samurai, and Vikings, who lived and breathed these principles. They adhered to strict codes of conduct, enduring rigorous training regimes, and often facing life-and-death situations. These soldiers were revered not just for their physical prowess but for their resilience and unyielding spirit. In modern times, the challenges we face have evolved. While we may no longer engage in physical combat, the battles have shifted to the boardrooms, sports fields, and personal endeavors. The essence of the warrior mindset, however, remains unchanged. It is about cultivating mental fortitude and a strategic approach to life's myriad challenges. Understanding its historical roots allows us to appreciate its timeless value. By examining how these principles have been adapted to contemporary settings, we can glean valuable insights into achieving peak performance in our own lives.

The Spartans of ancient Greece are perhaps the most iconic example of this discipline. Renowned for their toughness and military prowess, Spartans lived by a strict code that prioritized strength, loyalty, and sacrifice. From a young age, Spartan boys were enrolled in the agoge, a rigorous education and training program designed to instill resilience and endurance. They were taught to endure pain, hunger, and harsh conditions, ensuring that they could face any challenge. One of the most celebrated examples of Spartan discipline is the Battle of Thermopylae. As chronicled by the historian Herodotus, in 480 BCE, King Leonidas led a small contingent of 300 Spartans, along with a few thousand allied Greek soldiers, to defend the narrow pass of Thermopylae against the vastly superior Persian army. Despite being outnumbered, the Spartans held their ground for three days, using their strategic phalanx formation to inflict significant damage on the Persians. Their stand, though ultimately ending in their defeat, exemplified the Spartan virtues of discipline and sacrifice. The phrase "molon labe" ("come and take them"), reportedly spoken by Leonidas when asked to surrender their weapons, epitomizes their defiant spirit and unwavering commitment to their principles. The Spartan emphasis on willpower extended beyond the battlefield. Spartans practiced self-restraint in all aspects of life, from their austere lifestyle to their laconic speech, which was characterized by brevity and wit. This discipline created a culture where every action was purposeful, and every individual was committed to the greater good of the state. Another notable anecdote involves the Spartan practice of "krypteia.", a secret rite of passage for young Spartan males, where they were sent into the countryside with minimal supplies to survive and prove their worth. This practice not only tested their physical endurance and survival skills but also instilled a deep sense of self-reliance. These young Spartans learned to navigate and thrive in harsh conditions, embodying the discipline and toughness that were hallmarks of their culture.

The Samurai of feudal Japan represent another pinnacle of the soldier mindset. Guided by the Bushido code, which translates to "the way of the warrior," Samurai adhered to principles of honor, loyalty, and self-discipline. Bushido emphasized virtues such as courage, respect, and integrity, shaping Samurai conduct both in combat and in daily life. A notable example of Samurai toughness and loyalty is the tale of the Forty-seven Ronin. In 1701, their master, Asano Naganori, was forced to commit seppuku (ritual suicide) after assaulting a court official. The 47 samurai who served him became ronin (masterless samurai) and vowed to avenge their master's death. After two years of meticulous planning, they succeeded in killing the official, demonstrating extraordinary patience, strategy, and loyalty. Their actions, while resulting in their own eventual demise, are celebrated in Japanese culture as the epitome of Bushido and the Samurai spirit. Samurai training extended beyond martial skills to include arts, literature, and philosophy, fostering a well-rounded and disciplined individual. This holistic approach ensured that Samurai were not only formidable combatants but also cultured and principled leaders. Their commitment to continuous self-improvement and adherence to a strict moral code are lessons that resonate even today. The Samurai ethos of honor and loyalty is vividly illustrated in the tale of the Forty-seven Ronin. In 1701, Asano Naganori, a young daimyo (feudal lord), was provoked and subsequently punished by the shogunate for drawing his sword within Edo Castle. Forced to commit seppuku, Asano left behind a group of loyal samurai who became ronin (masterless samurai). For two years, these ronin meticulously planned their revenge against the court official responsible for their master's death. On a snowy night in 1703, they successfully avenged Asano by killing the official, an act that cost them their own lives as they too were ordered to commit seppuku. This story, immortalized in literature and theater, showcases the Samurai's unwavering commitment to honor, loyalty, and justice, even in the face of death. Another poignant example is found in the life of Miyamoto Musashi, one of Japan's most famous swordsmen and philosophers. Musashi, author of "The Book of Five Rings," was a master strategist and undefeated duelist. His approach to combat and life was deeply rooted in the principles of discipline and strategy. Musashi's concept of "Kenjutsu" (the art of the sword) extended beyond physical techniques to encompass mental and spiritual training. His famous duel with Sasaki Kojiro, where he arrived late and used a wooden sword to defeat his heavily armed opponent, exemplifies his strategic brilliance and psychological acumen. Musashi's life and writings continue to inspire martial artists and strategists worldwide.

The Vikings, seafaring Norse warriors from Scandinavia, are often depicted as fierce and ruthless raiders. However, their culture was also characterized by adaptability and a strong sense of community. Vikings navigated the harsh climates of the North Atlantic, demonstrating remarkable seafaring skills and strategic acumen. The Viking principle is exemplified in their exploration and settlement efforts. Viking sagas, such as the tale of Erik the Red, recount the hardships and perseverance of Norse settlers as they ventured to Greenland and beyond. Erik the Red, exiled from Iceland, led a group of settlers to Greenland, overcoming severe weather and treacherous seas. Their ability to adapt and thrive in such harsh environments speaks to their formidable ingenuity. Viking society was built on a foundation of honor and loyalty. The concept of "drengskapr," which encompasses bravery, loyalty, and integrity, guided their actions. Vikings were expected to show courage in battle and loyalty to their chieftains and comrades. The importance of these values is evident in the sagas and poems that celebrate their heroic deeds and feuds, where personal and familial honor were paramount. The adventurous spirit of the Vikings is captured in the sagas, epic narratives that recount their exploits and journeys. One such saga is "The Saga of Erik the Red," which tells the story of Erik Thorvaldsson, better known as Erik the Red. Exiled from Norway and later Iceland for his involvement in violent disputes, Erik set sail with his followers to find and colonize Greenland. Facing treacherous seas and harsh climates, Erik and his settlers demonstrated remarkable adaptability. Their successful establishment of settlements in Greenland stands as a testament to their indomitable spirit and pioneering resolve. Another compelling Viking story is that of Leif Erikson, Erik the Red's son, who is credited with being one of the first Europeans to reach North America, specifically the region he called Vinland (modern-day Newfoundland). According to "The Saga of the Greenlanders," Leif's journey was fraught with danger, including navigating unknown waters and encountering hostile indigenous peoples. Despite these challenges, Leif's strategic thinking and leadership enabled his crew to explore and establish a foothold in the New World, long before

Columbus. This tale of exploration highlights the Viking ability to overcome formidable obstacles through courage and ingenuity.

This mindset, deeply ingrained in the fabric of ancient civilizations, is built upon four foundational principles: discipline, honor, resilience, and strategy. These principles not only defined the lives and actions of historical champions, but also provided timeless lessons applicable to our modern lives. By examining these key principles in a discursive manner, we can better understand their significance and relevance today. **Discipline** forms the bedrock of this mindset. For the ancient Spartans, discipline was instilled from a young age through the agoge, a rigorous training regimen designed to cultivate physical strength, endurance, and perseverance. Spartan society valued discipline above all else, believing that a disciplined warrior was an effective one. This relentless commitment to self-control and order allowed the Spartans to achieve remarkable feats, such as their legendary stand at Thermopylae. In contemporary life, discipline remains a crucial virtue. Whether striving for professional success, personal growth, or physical fitness, maintaining discipline enables us to pursue our goals with focus and determination. It involves setting clear objectives, adhering to structured routines, and making sacrifices when necessary. Just as the Spartans endured physical and inner challenges to prepare for battle, we too must cultivate discipline to navigate the complexities of modern life and achieve our aspirations. **Honor** was the guiding force for many ancient troopers, serving as a moral compass that directed their actions and decisions. The Samurai of feudal Japan epitomized this principle through the Bushido code,

48

which emphasized virtues such as loyalty, integrity, and respect. Honor dictated not only how Samurai conducted themselves in battle but also how they interacted with others in their daily lives. The tale of the Forty-seven Ronin exemplifies the profound sense of honor that drove these brave people to avenge their master's unjust death, even at the cost of their own lives. In today's world, honor manifests as a commitment to ethical behavior and moral integrity. It involves upholding our values, keeping our promises, and treating others with respect and fairness. In professional settings, honor can be seen in maintaining honesty and transparency, even when faced with difficult choices. In personal relationships, it involves loyalty and sincerity. By embracing the principle of honor, we build trust and credibility, fostering meaningful connections and a strong sense of self-respect.

Strategic thinking is essential for effective action, a principle well understood by the men in history books. The Spartans' use of the phalanx formation, the Samurai's meticulous battle plans, and the Vikings' surprise raids all demonstrate the importance of strategy in achieving military success. These gladiators analyzed their strengths and weaknesses, understood their enemies, and crafted tactics that maximized their chances of victory. In the contemporary context, strategic thinking is crucial in both professional and personal realms. It involves setting long-term goals, anticipating potential challenges, and making informed decisions. Whether managing a business, planning a career, or navigating personal relationships, employing strategic thinking helps us achieve our objectives efficiently and effectively. It requires critical thinking, foresight, and the ability to adapt plans as circumstances change. By adopting a strategic approach, we can navigate the complexities of modern life with confidence and purpose. Whether you're striving for success in your career, facing personal challenges, or seeking to enhance your overall grit, the principles discussed in this chapter will serve as a valuable guide. In our often-chaotic world, we are all modern-day warriors. Our battlefields are no longer confined to distant lands or historical epochs; they are found in our workplaces, our homes, and within our own minds. The pressures of modern life—economic uncertainty, information overload, and the relentless pursuit of success—demand a level of willpower akin to that of ancient champions. Consider the professional arena, where competition is fierce, and the stakes are high. Whether you're navigating corporate hierarchies, striving for entrepreneurial success, or excelling in a creative field, the challenges are immense. Here, this mindset manifests as the ability to stay focused under pressure, adapt to rapidly changing circumstances, and persist despite setbacks. The willingness to recover from failures and the discipline to continuously improve are what set the modern champion apart. In our personal lives, we face battles of a different kind. From managing relationships and raising families to pursuing personal growth and maintaining health, these challenges require a different form of strength. Emotional balance, the capacity to manage stress, and the ability to find balance amidst chaos are critical. Like the ancient fighters who trained their minds and bodies, we too must cultivate a holistic approach to well-being. The digital age presents unique challenges that test our endurance. The constant barrage of information, the lure of social media, and the pressure to remain constantly connected can be overwhelming. Developing this kind of mindset in this context means honing the ability to filter distractions, maintain focus, and prioritize what truly matters. Being a modern warrior is about embodying the principles of discipline and strategic thinking in every aspect of life. It's about facing our challenges head-on, drawing strength from within, and persevering with unwavering determination. By adopting this mindset, we equip ourselves to navigate the complexities of modern life with courage and grace.

As previously mentioned, in today's world, this mindset has evolved to meet the demands of a rapidly changing environment. The traditional principles of discipline, honor and strategy, though rooted in ancient cultures, have found new expressions and applications in contemporary settings. As we navigate the complexities of modern life, these principles remain as relevant as ever, guiding us through technological advancements, a fast-paced lifestyle, and the ongoing quest for psychical and emotional well-being. Discipline, once forged in the rigorous training of ancient soldiers, now manifests in our ability to maintain focus and consistency amidst a barrage of distractions. In the age of smartphones and constant connectivity, the discipline to prioritize tasks, manage time effectively, and resist the lure of instant gratification is paramount. Professionals who excel in their fields often attribute their success to the disciplined routines they adhere to, whether it's dedicating time to continuous learning, maintaining physical fitness, or practicing mindfulness to enhance mental clarity. Honor, a concept deeply ingrained in the codes of the past, translates today into a commitment to ethical behavior and integrity. In the corporate world, leaders who embody honor build trust and foster a culture of accountability and respect. This modern interpretation extends beyond professional realms into personal interactions, where honor is demonstrated through authenticity, transparency, and a steadfast adherence to one's values, even in the face of adversity. Strategy, a cornerstone of ancient military success, is now essential in navigating the complexities of contemporary life. Strategic thinking involves setting long-term goals, anticipating obstacles, and making informed decisions. Whether it's in business, where market dynamics shift rapidly, or in personal development, where life plans need constant adjustment, strategic thinking empowers individuals to chart a clear path forward, maximizing opportunities and mitigating risks. The landscape of modern life is shaped by technological advancements and an unprecedented pace of change. These factors have introduced unique challenges that test our ability to maintain this mindset. Technological advancements, while providing numerous benefits, also contribute to information overload and heightened expectations. The constant stream of emails, notifications, and updates can overwhelm our cognitive resources, leading to decision fatigue and decreased productivity. The modern warrior must develop procedures to manage this deluge of information, such as setting boundaries for technology use, prioritizing deep work over multitasking, and employing digital detoxes to recharge mentally. The fast-paced nature of contemporary life often leaves little room for reflection and rest. The pressure to constantly perform and achieve can lead to burnout, a state of physical and emotional exhaustion. To counteract this, the modern gladiator emphasizes the importance of balance and self-care. Incorporating regular breaks, practicing understanding and ensuring adequate sleep are essential practices that help maintain peak performance and prevent burnout. The interconnectedness of our world means that challenges are no longer isolated. Economic downturns, global health crises, and environmental issues can have far-reaching impacts, requiring a collective steadfastness and adaptive response. He or she understands the importance of community and collaboration, leveraging social support and shared resources to navigate these complex challenges.

As we adapt to the demands of modern life, our understanding of psychical and emotional well-being has deepened. Traditional notions of stoicism and endurance have evolved into a more nuanced appreciation of psychological flexibility and emotional intelligence. Psychological flexibility, the ability to adapt one's thinking and behavior in response to changing circumstances, is a key component of this. It involves being open to new experiences, maintaining a growth mindset, and being willing to adjust goals and strategies as needed. It contrasts with rigid thinking patterns that can hinder progress and lead to unnecessary stress. Emotional intelligence, the capacity to understand and manage one's emotions, is another crucial aspect. This includes self-awareness, empathy, and effective communication. In high-pressure environments, emotional intelligence enables individuals to remain calm, make sound decisions, and build strong relationships. Techniques such as meditation, journaling, and emotional regulation exercises can enhance emotional intelligence, providing a solid foundation. Additionally, the role of mental health has gained greater recognition. Unlike the ancient champions who often faced physical threats, modern challenges frequently manifest as psychological stressors. Acknowledging its impact and seeking appropriate support—whether through therapy, counseling, or peer support groups—are vital. In the workplace, fostering a culture that supports mental health can lead to more engaged and productive teams. This includes implementing policies that promote work-life balance, providing access to psychological resources, and encouraging open discussions about stress and coping approach. By creating environments where individuals feel valued and supported, organizations can enhance overall equilibrium and performance.

From military personnel to athletes and business leaders, contemporary warriors demonstrate these principles through their actions and achievements. Here, we explore the profiles of a few such individuals, highlighting how they embody this mindset and the lessons we can learn from their experiences. **Admiral William H. McRaven**, a retired U.S. Navy SEAL and former Commander of U.S. Special Operations Command, exemplifies this way of approaching life through his distinguished military career. Known for his leadership in the operation that led to the death of Osama bin Laden, McRaven's approach to discipline and strategy offers valuable insights. One of McRaven's most famous contributions is his commencement speech at the University of Texas at Austin in 2014, where he outlined life lessons derived from Navy SEAL training. His first piece of advice— "Make your bed every morning"—illustrates the importance of discipline and attention to detail. This simple act sets a positive tone for the day, instilling a sense of accomplishment and order. McRaven's career is also marked by his toughness in the face of adversity. Navy SEAL training, known as one of the most grueling military programs, demands physical and psychical elasticity. McRaven's ability to endure this rigorous training and later lead complex missions underlines the importance of perseverance and adaptability. **Serena Williams**, widely regarded as one of the greatest tennis players of all time, embodies the champion mindset through her dedication, perseverance, and strategic approach to the game. Williams has won 23 Grand Slam singles titles, demonstrating an extraordinary level of discipline and excellence. Williams' training regimen is a testament to her discipline. Her rigorous practice schedule, commitment to fitness, and continuous improvement have kept her at the top of her sport for over two decades. Despite numerous injuries and personal challenges, Williams' strength has allowed her to maintain peak performance and return to competition stronger each time. Her determination is evident in her ability to handle pressure during high-stakes matches. Williams often speaks about the importance of maintaining focus and composure, even when faced with adversity. Her strategic mindset is clear in her gameplay, where she adapts her tactics to outmaneuver opponents, showcasing her deep understanding of the sport. **Elon Musk**, the CEO of SpaceX and

Tesla, exemplifies this mindset in the business world through his visionary leadership and strategic thinking in the face of challenges. Musk's ability to revolutionize industries and drive innovation highlights the principles of the lessons we learned here. Musk's discipline is reflected in his work ethic and commitment to his vision. He is known for working long hours and maintaining a hands-on approach to his ventures. This level of dedication has been instrumental in achieving groundbreaking advancements in space exploration and electric vehicles. From the early struggles of SpaceX, which faced multiple failed launches, to the financial difficulties at Tesla, Musk has demonstrated an unwavering determination to overcome obstacles. His ability to persist through setbacks and learn from failures has been critical to his success. Strategically, Musk excels in identifying opportunities and executing long-term plans. His ambitious goals, such as colonizing Mars and transitioning to sustainable energy, require meticulous planning and a deep understanding of technology and market dynamics. Musk's strategic vision and ability to rally teams around his ideas showcase the power of strategic thinking in achieving monumental goals. **Dr. Atul Gawande**, a renowned surgeon, writer, and public health researcher, exemplifies this strong mindset in the field of medicine. Gawande's discipline is evident in his meticulous approach to surgery and his dedication to continuous improvement. He advocates for the use of checklists in surgical procedures to enhance safety and reduce errors. This methodical approach reflects a commitment to precision and excellence. Discipline is a key theme in Gawande's work, especially in his efforts to address complex healthcare challenges. His book, "Being Mortal," explores the difficult realities of aging and end-of-life care, emphasizing the need for compassionate and resilient approaches in medicine. Gawande's ability to tackle tough issues and propose practical solutions underscores his cleverness. Strategically, Gawande excels in translating research into actionable improvements in healthcare. His initiatives, such as the World Health Organization's Surgical Safety Checklist, demonstrate how strategic thinking can lead to significant advancements in patient safety and quality of care. Gawande's strategic mindset drives systemic changes that benefit countless patients.

These individuals, from diverse fields, demonstrate that this mindset is not confined to the battlefield but is applicable in various aspects of modern life. Their stories provide valuable lessons in achieving excellence, overcoming adversity, and pursuing visionary goals. By adopting these principles, we can navigate our own challenges with the strength and determination of a true warrior.

My brother Michael's journey has been a profound source of inspiration and a vivid illustration of what we are talking about. His unwavering determination and strategic approach to overcoming adversity have deeply influenced my views and teachings on the matter. Michael's determination was evident in every aspect of his recovery process. One particular moment stands out: during his early rehabilitation days, the simple task of sitting upright unaided for even a few minutes was a monumental challenge. Instead of succumbing to frustration, Michael approached this task with the precision and discipline of a seasoned fighter. He broke the task down into manageable steps, first mastering the ability to balance himself for a few seconds and gradually increasing the duration. His patience and persistence were reminiscent of the Samurai's meticulous training, where mastery is achieved through incremental progress and unwavering focus. Another powerful example of Michael's determination was his commitment to regaining mobility through adaptive sports. Initially, the idea of participating in wheelchair basketball seemed daunting. Yet, Michael approached it with a strategic mindset, understanding that physical strength and coordination would not return overnight. He dedicated himself to the sport, attending practice sessions, and pushing his physical limits. Over time, his hard work paid off, and he became an integral part of the team. His journey in adaptive sports demonstrated a strongness akin to the Vikings' adaptability and perseverance in uncharted territories. Michael's approach to his new reality also embodied the principle of honor. Despite the dramatic change in his circumstances, he never allowed his situation to define his self-worth or his contribution to society. He continued to engage in community service, mentoring others facing similar challenges, and sharing his story to inspire and motivate. His integrity and commitment to helping others reflected the honor that was paramount in the lives of ancient warriors. Witnessing Michael's journey firsthand has had a profound impact on my perspective and teachings. His experience has reinforced my belief in the power of flexibility and the importance of maintaining a strategic approach to life's challenges. Michael's ability to set realistic goals, break them down into achievable steps, and remain steadfast in the face of adversity has become a cornerstone of my teachings. Michael's journey has highlighted the significance of community and support networks. His progress was not achieved in isolation but with the help of family, friends, medical professionals, and fellow athletes. This communal support mirrored the collective strength seen in historical military societies, where camaraderie and mutual support were essential for survival and success. It reinforced the idea that, while individual determination is crucial, the support of a community can amplify one's psychical and physical strength. Michael's story has also deepened my understanding of honor in the modern context. His unwavering commitment to living with integrity, helping others, and maintaining a positive outlook despite his circumstances has shown me that honor is not just about personal achievements but also about contributing to the greater good. This insight has shaped my teachings, emphasizing that this mindset involves not only personal stability and strategy but also a commitment to ethical behavior and community service.

Michael's discipline during his rehabilitation was a powerful reminder of the importance of consistent effort and focus. Watching him break down seemingly insurmountable tasks into manageable steps and tackle them one by one was incredibly motivating. I applied this principle to my work, especially during demanding projects or when faced with tight deadlines. By setting clear, incremental goals and maintaining discipline, I found that I could achieve higher levels of productivity and quality in my work. Michael's toughness in the face of adversity was perhaps the most profound lesson. His ability to remain positive and proactive, despite the physical and emotional challenges he faced, taught me the value of perseverance. In my career, there have been numerous setbacks and obstacles, from failed ventures to professional rejections. Drawing inspiration from Michael, I learned to view these setbacks not as insurmountable barriers but as opportunities for growth and learning. This shift in perspective allowed me to recover quickly from failures, adapt to changing circumstances, and continue striving toward my goals with renewed vigor. Michael's strategic approach to his recovery, particularly his involvement in adaptive sports, highlighted the importance of planning and adaptability. In my professional life, I began to place greater emphasis on strategic thinking. Whether developing business plans, executing projects, or navigating complex negotiations, I adopted a more thoughtful and strategic approach. This not only improved my decision-making but also enhanced my ability to foresee and mitigate potential risks, leading to more successful outcomes. Michael's unwavering commitment to honor and integrity influenced my interactions with colleagues, clients, and partners. His example underscored the importance of ethical behavior and maintaining a strong moral compass, even when faced with difficult choices. By upholding these values in my professional dealings, I built stronger relationships based on trust and respect. This, in turn, opened up new opportunities and collaborations, furthering my success. My brother's story has also inspired me in my role as a mentor and educator. His journey has provided a rich source of personal anecdotes and lessons that I share with those I mentor. By illustrating the principles of discipline, strategy, and honor through his experiences, I can offer more relatable and impactful guidance. This has not only enriched my teaching but also allowed me to inspire and motivate others to adopt a warrior mindset in their own lives.

The Science of Resilience and Performance

Understanding resilience and performance requires a deep dive into the fields of neuroscience and psychology. These disciplines offer critical insights into how our brains and minds adapt, learn, and excel, especially under pressure. Neuroscience explores the structure and function of the brain, revealing how neural pathways form and change in response to experiences and challenges. This is where it all begins: in the brain's ability to adapt and reorganize itself, known as neuroplasticity. Psychology, on the other hand, provides a framework for understanding the psychological processes. Concepts such as grit, growth mindset, and emotional regulation are essential for developing a resilient mindset and achieving peak performance. By integrating the latest findings from these fields, we can develop more effective planning for enhancing our grit and ability to perform under pressure. In "The Art of Impossible," Steven Kotler delves into the neuroscience behind peak performance, offering insights into how we can push our limits and achieve the seemingly impossible. Similarly, Jim Kwik's "Limitless" explores the practical applications of neuroscience and psychology to unlock our brain's full potential. Both of these works provide invaluable context and support for the principles discussed in this chapter. As we explore recent discoveries in neuroscience and psychology, we'll uncover practical applications that can be integrated into our daily lives. Resilience, often described as the ability to bounce back from adversity, begins in the brain. Neuroscience has provided us with a wealth of knowledge about how our brains respond to stress, adapt to challenges, and ultimately, build it. At the core of this process is neuroplasticity—the brain's remarkable ability to reorganize itself by forming new neural connections throughout life. This adaptability is absolutely imperative. When we encounter a challenging situation, our brain's response involves several key areas, including the prefrontal cortex, the amygdala, and the hippocampus. The prefrontal cortex, responsible for executive functions such as decision-making and problem-solving, helps us to assess and respond to stressors. The amygdala, which processes emotions, triggers the fight-or-flight response. The hippocampus, involved in memory formation, allows us to learn from past experiences and apply those lessons to future challenges. Neuroplasticity, also known as brain plasticity, refers to the brain's ability to reorganize itself by forming new neural connections throughout life. This capacity for change is fundamental to learning, memory, and recovery from brain injuries. Neuroplasticity allows the brain to adapt to new situations, experiences, and environments by strengthening or weakening synapses—the connections between neurons. There are two primary types of neuroplasticity: structural and functional. Structural plasticity involves changes in the physical structure of the brain, such as the growth of new neurons (neurogenesis) or the formation of new synaptic connections. Functional plasticity refers to the brain's ability to move functions from damaged areas to undamaged areas, ensuring that essential cognitive processes continue even after injury. The brain's plasticity is influenced by various factors, including age, experience, and environment. For instance, engaging in new and challenging activities can enhance neuroplasticity, leading to improved cognitive abilities. Practices such as deliberate practice and continuous learning are known to promote neuroplasticity, helping individuals adapt to change and recover from setbacks more effectively. In essence, neuroplasticity is the brain's way of constantly evolving and improving its function, providing a foundation for adaptability and peak performance in the face of life's challenges. One of its most fascinating aspects is how neural pathways are formed and strengthened through repeated exposure to challenges. Each time we encounter and overcome a stressor; our brain reinforces the neural circuits associated with that experience. Over time, this process makes us more adept at handling similar situations in the future. Steven Kotler, in "The Art of Impossible," highlights this by explaining how repeated practice and pushing one's limits lead to the strengthening of these neural pathways. Kotler points out that resilience is not just about surviving adversity but thriving because of it. He cites research on elite athletes and top performers who consistently push themselves beyond their comfort zones. These individuals leverage neuroplasticity to their advantage, deliberately exposing themselves to controlled stressors to build tenacity. This process, known as deliberate practice, involves setting specific, challenging goals, receiving immediate feedback, and continually adjusting strategies to improve performance.

A study published in "Nature Reviews Neuroscience" supports Kotler's observations by demonstrating that individuals who engage in deliberate practice show significant changes in brain structure and function. The researchers found that these changes are particularly pronounced in areas related to cognitive control and emotional regulation, which are critical aspects of this field. In practical terms, building endurance through neuroplasticity involves adopting a mindset of continuous growth and learning. By embracing challenges and viewing failures as opportunities for growth, we can train our brains to become more resilient. It can be enhanced through meditation practices, which have been shown to promote neuroplasticity. Mindfulness helps regulate the amygdala's response to stress and enhances the prefrontal cortex's ability to manage emotional reactions.

Building on our understanding of neuroplasticity, it's clear that this dynamic capability of the brain plays a crucial role in performance enhancement. The brain's ability to adapt and reorganize itself provides the foundation for improving skills and abilities, which is essential for achieving peak performance in any field. Neuroplasticity's significance in performance improvement lies in its capacity to strengthen neural pathways through practice and learning. This means that with consistent effort and the right procedure, anyone can enhance their cognitive and physical skills. For instance, musicians and athletes often exhibit highly developed areas of the brain related to their specific skills due to years of dedicated practice. This targeted development is a direct result of neuroplasticity at work. Jim Kwik's "Limitless" delves into practical applications of neuroplasticity for unlocking our brain's full potential. Kwik emphasizes that by understanding and leveraging neuroplasticity, we can accelerate learning, improve memory, and boost cognitive performance. He outlines several key strategies that harness neuroplasticity for performance enhancement: **deliberate practice** involves focused, intentional practice aimed at improving specific aspects of a skill. Unlike regular practice, deliberate practice requires setting clear goals, receiving immediate feedback, and continually pushing beyond one's comfort zone. For example, a pianist might focus on mastering a particularly challenging piece by breaking it down into smaller sections, practicing each section repeatedly, and gradually increasing the tempo. **Visualization and emotional rehearsal** can strengthen neural pathways in much the same way physical practice does. Athletes often use this technique to enhance their performance. By vividly imagining themselves performing a skill successfully, they activate the same neural circuits involved in the actual execution of the skill. This inner practice helps to reinforce and optimize these neural pathways, leading to improved performance. Maintaining focus and practicing **mindfulness** can significantly enhance neuroplasticity. Meditation, for instance, has been shown to increase the thickness of the prefrontal cortex, which is associated with higher-order brain functions such as attention and decision-making. By improving our ability to concentrate, we can perform tasks more efficiently and effectively. Engaging in **continuous learning** keeps the brain active and promotes neuroplasticity. This doesn't just mean formal education; it can include learning new languages, playing a musical instrument, or even picking up a new hobby. By constantly challenging the brain with new information and experiences, we can enhance cognitive flexibility and overall brain function. **Physical activity** is not only beneficial for the body but also for the brain. Exercise has been shown to promote the growth of new neurons and enhance synaptic plasticity, particularly in areas related to learning and memory. Regular physical exercise can therefore improve cognitive performance. These schemes highlight how neuroplasticity can be harnessed to enhance skills and abilities. By incorporating deliberate practice, emotional rehearsal, continuous learning, and physical exercise into our routines, we can optimize our brain's potential and achieve greater performance levels. In conclusion, neuroplasticity is a powerful tool for performance enhancement. Understanding and leveraging this natural capability of the brain allows us to continually improve our skills and abilities. As "Limitless" illustrates, with the right mindset, we can unlock our brain's full potential, paving the way for exceptional performance in all areas of life.

Understanding these psychological principles provides valuable insights into how we can cultivate this crucial trait. This is not merely about bouncing back from adversity but also about growing stronger through challenges. Several key psychological concepts contribute to building it, including grit, growth mindset, and emotional regulation. **Grit** is a term popularized by psychologist Angela Duckworth, describing a combination of passion and perseverance for long-term goals. Sustained effort over time, rather than innate talent, often leads to extraordinary achievements. Grit involves maintaining effort and interest over years despite failures, setbacks, and plateaus. This persistence allows individuals to push through obstacles and continue striving toward their goals. **Growth mindset**, a concept developed by psychologist Carol Dweck, refers to the belief that abilities and intelligence can be developed through dedication and hard work. Viewing challenges as opportunities for growth rather than insurmountable obstacles fosters strength. When individuals believe they can improve and learn from their experiences, they are more likely to persevere in the face of adversity. This mindset shift transforms setbacks into valuable learning experiences, contributing to long-term steadfastness and success. **Emotional regulation** is another critical component. The ability to manage and respond to intense emotions in a healthy and adaptive way allows individuals to navigate stress and recover from difficult experiences more effectively. Emotional regulation involves skills such as mindfulness, cognitive reappraisal, and stress management techniques. Practicing awareness helps individuals stay focused and maintain emotional control under pressure. **Cognitive reappraisal**, a strategy where individuals change their interpretation of a potentially stress-inducing situation, is another effective emotional regulation technique. By reframing a challenge as an opportunity or viewing a setback as a temporary obstacle, individuals can reduce their emotional distress and approach problems more constructively. Changing our mental narratives can significantly impact our emotional. Developing strength through these psychological principles often involves cultivating supportive relationships and a sense of purpose. Strong social connections provide emotional support and practical assistance during difficult times, enhancing our capacity to cope with stress.

Additionally, having a clear sense of purpose and direction can motivate individuals to persist through challenges and maintain their flexibility. Aligning personal goals with a broader mission can provide a powerful source of motivation. Embracing these ideas allows us to transform challenges into opportunities for growth, fostering a resilient mindset that is essential for long-term success and well-being.

Regular **physical exercise** promotes neuroplasticity and enhances cognitive function. Activities such as aerobic exercise, strength training, and yoga have been shown to stimulate the growth of new neurons and improve brain health. Incorporate physical activity into your daily routine by setting aside time for workouts, taking regular breaks to move around, and choosing active forms of transportation, like walking or cycling. Exercise not only boosts physical health but also improves mood and overall well-being. Keeping your brain engaged with **continuous learning and emotional challenges** fosters neuroplasticity. Pursue hobbies that require skill and concentration, such as playing a musical instrument, solving puzzles, or learning a new craft. Regularly challenge your brain with new and complex tasks to maintain cognitive flexibility.

In this section, we have explored the fundamental role of neuroscience and psychology in understanding and enhancing resilience and performance. We began by discussing how the brain's remarkable ability to reorganize itself—known as neuroplasticity—forms its foundation. Through repeated exposure to challenges, our neural pathways are strengthened, allowing us to better handle similar situations in the future. These methods leverage the brain's adaptability to improve cognitive and physical performance. By understanding and applying these psychological principles, individuals can develop a resilient mindset, enabling them to thrive in the face of adversity. Systems like cognitive reappraisal and leveraging social support further enhance our ability to manage stress and maintain emotional balance. In practical terms, integrating these insights into daily life involves adopting specific strategies to build perseverance, improve emotional regulation, and enhance overall well-being. Whether through focused practice, awareness exercises, or continuous learning, these applications provide powerful tools for developing and achieving peak performance. As we move forward, the next section will delve deeper into practical applications tailored by my own insights and experiences. By sharing personal anecdotes and original ideas, I will illustrate how these principles can be effectively applied to real-life scenarios.

Having explored the scientific foundations of this field, it's time to transition from theory to practice. The principles of neuroscience and psychology provide a robust framework, but their true power lies in practical application. In this section, I will share personal insights and experiences that have shaped my understanding of these concepts, demonstrating how they can be integrated into daily life. My journey toward developing a resilient mindset has been profoundly influenced by real-life challenges and triumphs. With over 20 years of experience as a consultant, I have had the privilege of working with high-profile organizations, including the military, professional sports teams, and major corporations. These experiences have taught me invaluable lessons about willpower, emotional regulation, focus, and motivation. In addition to my professional background, my personal experiences have also played a significant role in shaping my approach to life itself. Supporting my brother through his recovery after a life-changing accident has provided me with unique insights into the practical application of these principles. Each practical application discussed will be backed by personal anecdotes, illustrating how these modus operandi have been successfully implemented in various scenarios. Whether you are looking to enhance your emotional well-being, manage stress more effectively, or achieve peak performance, the upcoming content will offer actionable policies that are both effective and relatable. It is the ability to remain focused and composed under pressure, to persist through difficulties, and to bounce back from setbacks stronger than before. Building grit requires consistent effort and intentional practices. Here, I will share ideas for developing strength of mind, supported by personal anecdotes from my life. One of the most effective ways to build it is by embracing challenges rather than avoiding them. This means seeking out opportunities that push you out of your comfort zone. When I was consulting for a military unit, I witnessed firsthand how soldiers deliberately put themselves in challenging situations during training. They would simulate high-pressure scenarios to prepare for real combat. By regularly facing and overcoming these challenges, they built an incredible level of tenacity. In my own life, I've taken on endurance sports such as marathons and triathlons. Training for these events requires long hours of physical and psychical exertion. There were days when my body wanted to quit, but pushing through those moments of doubt strengthened my resolve and determination. Each finish line crossed was a testament to the power of perseverance. During stressful periods of my career, particularly when working with high-stakes corporate clients, I found that daily meditation sessions helped me maintain clarity and composure. One particular instance stands out when I was preparing a presentation for a major corporation. The stakes were high, and the pressure was immense. By incorporating mindfulness methods, such as deep-breathing exercises and guided meditation, I was able to calm my mind and deliver the presentation with confidence. Setting and achieving incremental goals can significantly boost stamina. Breaking down larger objectives into smaller, manageable tasks makes it easier to stay motivated and measure progress. When my brother was recovering from his accident, the road to recovery seemed daunting. We set small, achievable goals for his rehabilitation process, celebrating each milestone along the way. This approach not only kept his spirits high but also reinforced the importance of persistence and incremental progress. Adopting a growth mindset—the belief that abilities and intelligence can be developed through effort and learning—is crucial for tenacity. During my tenure as a performance coach, I emphasized this mindset with my clients, encouraging them to learn from their mistakes and keep pushing forward. A personal experience that highlights this is when I faced a major professional setback early in my career. Instead of seeing it as a failure, I viewed it as a learning opportunity. This perspective allowed me to bounce back, refine my skills, and eventually achieve greater success. Having a strong support system is essential for developing grit. Surrounding yourself with positive, encouraging individuals can provide the motivation and support needed to persevere through tough times. Throughout my career and personal life, I have been fortunate to have a network of family, friends, and colleagues who have supported me. Their encouragement and advice have been invaluable, particularly during challenging periods.

Emotional regulation is the ability to manage and respond to emotional experiences in a healthy and adaptive way. It's a critical component of this field, helping us maintain composure and clarity even under stress. Here are some practical ways for managing emotions and reducing stress, along with personal anecdotes illustrating their effectiveness. Mindfulness meditation involves focusing on the present moment without judgment. This practice can help reduce stress and increase emotional regulation by creating a space between stimulus and response. During particularly stressful periods of my career, I turned to this to maintain my emotional balance. One memorable instance was during a high-pressure consulting project with a top-level sports team. The stakes were incredibly high, and the pressure was mounting as we approached a critical phase. I started each day with a 15-minute meditation session, focusing on my breath and observing my thoughts without attachment. This practice not only helped me manage my stress levels but also improved my focus and decision-making abilities, ultimately contributing to the project's success. Cognitive reappraisal involves changing the way we interpret and respond to stress-inducing situations. By reframing negative or challenging experiences in a more positive light, we can reduce their emotional impact. A powerful example of cognitive reappraisal in my life occurred when I faced a significant professional setback. Early in my career, I was passed over for a promotion I had worked tirelessly for. Initially, I felt devastated and questioned my abilities. However, by reappraising the situation, I began to see it as an opportunity for growth and improvement. I identified areas where I could enhance my skills and took proactive steps to develop them. This positive reframing helped me stay motivated and eventually led to greater career advancements. Deep-breathing exercises are a simple yet effective way to regulate emotions and reduce stress. These exercises involve taking slow, deep breaths to activate the body's relaxation response. I frequently use deep-breathing techniques before high-stakes presentations or meetings. One particularly stressful event was a keynote speech at a conference. Moments before stepping on stage, I felt a wave of anxiety. I took a few minutes to practice deep-breathing exercises, inhaling deeply through my nose, holding my breath for a few seconds, and then exhaling slowly through my mouth. This simple technique calmed my nerves, allowing me to deliver a confident and composed speech. Physical exercise is another powerful tool for emotional regulation. Regular exercise can help reduce stress, improve mood, and enhance overall emotional well-being. During my brother's recovery from his accident, we incorporated physical exercise into his rehabilitation routine. Despite the wellness and emotional challenges, he faced, engaging in regular exercise helped boost his mood and provided a healthy outlet for stress. We started with light activities such as walking and gradually increased the intensity as his strength improved. This not only aided his physical recovery but also significantly improved his emotional balance. Journaling involves writing down thoughts and feelings to gain clarity and perspective. This practice can help process emotions, reduce stress, and enhance self-awareness. I adopted journaling as a daily habit during a particularly challenging phase of my career. Balancing multiple high-pressure projects left me feeling overwhelmed and emotionally drained. By setting aside time each evening to journal, I was able to reflect on the day's events, process my emotions, and identify patterns or triggers contributing to my stress. This practice provided a valuable outlet for my feelings and helped me develop more effective coping strategies.

Enhancing focus and attention is crucial for achieving peak performance. Developing the ability to concentrate deeply on tasks can significantly improve productivity and overall well-being. Here are some effective tips and exercises to improve concentration and reduce distractions, along with examples from my professional journey where enhanced focus made a significant difference. One of the simplest yet most effective ways to improve focus is to create an environment conducive to concentration. This means eliminating potential distractions, such as unnecessary electronics, clutter, and noise. During my time consulting for high-profile corporate clients, I noticed a significant improvement in my focus when I worked in a clean, organized space free from distractions. For instance, before diving into complex strategic planning sessions, I would clear my desk of any non-essential items and ensure my workspace was quiet and comfortable. This practice helped me maintain a high level of concentration and productivity. The Pomodoro Technique involves breaking work into intervals, usually 25 minutes long, separated by short breaks. This method helps maintain sustained focus and prevent burnout. I discovered the Pomodoro Technique while working on a demanding project that required intense concentration for extended periods. By using a timer to structure my work sessions, I found that I could stay focused for longer durations without feeling overwhelmed. After each 25-minute session, I would take a five-minute break to stretch, walk around, or engage in a brief relaxation exercise. This approach kept my mind fresh and my productivity high. Setting clear, specific goals and prioritizing tasks can greatly enhance focus. Knowing exactly what needs to be accomplished and tackling tasks in order of importance helps prevent procrastination and keeps attention directed toward critical activities. During a high-stakes project with a professional sports team, I implemented this strategy by creating a detailed action plan with prioritized tasks and deadlines. This clear roadmap kept me on track and ensured that I dedicated my focus to the most important aspects of the project. Taking regular breaks is essential for maintaining focus and preventing mental fatigue. Short breaks allow the brain to rest and recharge, leading to better concentration during work periods. While working on an intense consulting project for a government agency, I scheduled short breaks throughout my day to prevent burnout. These breaks included stepping outside for fresh air, doing a few stretches, or simply closing my eyes for a few minutes. These brief respites helped me maintain a high level of focus and efficiency. Multitasking can significantly reduce focus and productivity. Instead, focus on one task at a time to improve concentration and the quality of work. Early in my career, I learned the pitfalls of multitasking while juggling multiple client projects simultaneously. By shifting my approach to focus on one project at a time, I noticed a marked improvement in the quality of my work and my ability to concentrate. Several tools and apps are designed to enhance focus and productivity. Tools like noise-canceling headphones, focus apps, and website blockers can help minimize distractions and improve concentration. For example, while writing my book, I used a website blocker to restrict access to distracting sites and noise-canceling headphones to create a quiet environment. These tools were invaluable in helping me maintain focus during long writing sessions. Sustaining motivation over long periods can be challenging, but it is essential for achieving long-term goals and maintaining high performance. Here are some effective methods for building and maintaining motivation, along with personal anecdotes from my journey. Setting clear, achievable goals provides direction and purpose, which are crucial for maintaining motivation. Breaking down larger objectives into smaller, manageable tasks can make them less overwhelming and more attainable. Reflect on why a particular goal is important to you and how it aligns with your values and long-term vision. When my brother faced a life-changing accident, supporting his recovery became my primary motivation. Seeing his determination and progress inspired me to push through my own challenges and stay focused on my work, knowing that my efforts could make a meaningful difference in his life. Celebrating small wins along the way can help maintain motivation by providing a sense of accomplishment and progress. During a particularly demanding consulting project for a major corporation, I implemented a system of rewarding myself for meeting intermediate milestones. Whether it was taking a short break, enjoying a favorite treat, or spending time with family, these small rewards kept my spirits high and motivation strong. Passion fuels motivation. Engaging in activities that you are passionate about can help sustain long-term motivation. My passion for endurance sports has been a constant source of motivation in both my personal and professional life. Training for marathons and triathlons taught me the importance of dedication, perseverance, and the joy of achieving challenging goals. This passion translates into my work, where I strive to help others reach their peak performance. Having a strong support network can boost motivation by providing encouragement, accountability, and perspective. Throughout my career, I have been fortunate to have mentors, colleagues, and friends who supported and believed in me. Their encouragement during tough times and their willingness to celebrate my successes have been invaluable in maintaining my motivation. Visualization is a powerful technique for maintaining motivation. By vividly imagining the successful achievement of your goals, you can reinforce your commitment and drive. Before major presentations or projects, I spend a few minutes visualizing a positive outcome. This practice not only boosts my confidence but also strengthens my resolve to achieve my objectives.

These aren't just lofty ideas—they're practical, actionable steps you can weave into your daily routine to become a true champion in life's battles. We talked about embracing challenges like a champ, practicing mindfulness to keep your cool, setting and crushing those incremental goals, and adopting a growth mindset that says, "Bring it on!" Emotional regulation? You've got tools like meditation, cognitive reappraisal, deep-breathing exercises, physical workouts, and even good old journaling to keep those emotions in check and stress at bay. Enhancing focus means creating a distraction-free zone, rocking the Pomodoro Technique, setting clear goals, and practicing consciousness to stay in the zone. And when it comes to motivation, it's all about knowing your "why," celebrating those small wins, staying passionate, surrounding yourself with your personal cheer squad, and visualizing your success. But we're just getting started. The next sections will take you deeper into the art of resilience. Get ready for advanced techniques, cutting-edge recovery and regeneration methods, powerful emotional schemes, and tips for continuous excellence. These upcoming chapters are packed with insights to elevate your game to new heights. Buckle up, because we're about to turn you into an unstoppable force, ready to tackle any challenge life throws your way. Let's go!

Part II: Developing Next-Level Resilience

Dynamic Resilience

In today's world, uncertainty has become the new normal. From economic fluctuations to rapid technological advancements, the landscape of our lives is constantly shifting beneath our feet. It's as if we're all trying to balance on a tightrope, with gusts of change threatening to throw us off at any moment. But instead of succumbing to the chaos, what if we could harness this uncertainty to build a stronger, more resilient mindset? Consider this: the very fabric of our daily existence is woven with unpredictability. Whether it's a sudden job change, an unexpected health scare, or even the daily bombardment of information from countless digital sources, uncertainty is an inescapable part of our reality. Yet, it's not the uncertainty itself that determines our success or failure, but how we respond to it. This is where the Warrior Mindset 2.0 comes into play. To thrive in this modern age, we need to redefine our approach to resilience. Gone are the days when brute strength and sheer willpower were enough to overcome life's challenges. Today, we need a dynamic set of tools that allow us to adapt and excel, no matter what curveballs life throws our way. One of the first steps in dealing with uncertainty is acknowledging its inevitability. It's like acknowledging the weather – we can't control it, but we can certainly prepare for it. The key is to develop a proactive mindset that anticipates change and prepares for it, rather than being caught off guard. Let's think about the unpredictability of technological advancements. Just a few decades ago, no one could have predicted the impact of smartphones and social media on our daily lives. Today, these technologies dictate how we communicate, work, and even think. By staying flexible and open to new developments, we can navigate these changes more effectively. Embracing uncertainty involves cultivating a sense of curiosity and openness. Instead of viewing the unknown as a threat, we can see it as a field of possibilities. This shift in perspective can transform our approach to challenges, making us more innovative and resourceful. For instance, rather than dreading a new job role, think of it as an opportunity to learn new skills and expand your professional network. In essence, developing a Warrior Mindset 2.0 isn't about eliminating uncertainty; it's about learning to dance with it. It's about cultivating a mindset that not only withstands the storms but also finds strength and opportunity within them. This requires a blend of brain agility, emotional intelligence, and practical policies. In the following sections, we'll delve into specifics and habits that can help you manage uncertainty effectively. Drawing lightly on insights from James Clear's "Atomic Habits," we'll explore how small, incremental changes in behavior can lead to significant improvements in how we handle the unpredictable nature of life. But more importantly, we'll weave in personal anecdotes and lessons from my own journey, showing you that this isn't just a concept—it's a way of life.

So, buckle up and get ready to transform your relationship with uncertainty. The path ahead may be unpredictable, but with the right mindset, it can also be incredibly rewarding.

Understanding that uncertainty is an inevitable part of life allows us to approach it with a sense of curiosity and openness rather than fear. When we view uncertainty as a natural state, we start to see it less as a threat and more as a blank canvas full of potential. This shift in mindset is not about being blindly optimistic but about being realistically hopeful and resourceful. Research from the past few years has shown that those who excel in uncertain environments often employ adaptive schemes. These procedures include maintaining inner flexibility, being open to new information, and adjusting plans as new data emerges. For instance, a 2020 study in the *Journal of Organizational Behavior* found that employees who regularly reassessed their goals and programs in response to changing conditions were more successful and satisfied in their roles. Psychological flexibility—the ability to remain present and engaged while adapting to changing circumstances—is another key component in handling uncertainty. Studies, such as the one published in *Behavior Research and Therapy* in 2021, highlight that individuals with high psychological flexibility can better manage stress and maintain higher levels of performance under pressure. The role of social support cannot be underestimated. Engaging with a supportive network of friends, family, and colleagues provides a buffer against the stresses of uncertainty. Research has consistently shown that social connections improve our ability to cope with stress and foster a sense of belonging and security. For example, a study published in *Psychological Science* in 2020 found that people with strong social ties were more resilient and better able to handle life's unpredictable nature. Adopting a mindset of continuous learning and growth helps us stay agile and prepared for whatever comes our way. The concept of lifelong learning encourages us to seek new knowledge and skills continually. This not only keeps us adaptable but also equips us with the tools to navigate new challenges effectively. Embracing a learner's mindset means welcoming mistakes and failures as part of the learning process, thereby reducing the fear of the unknown. Incorporating these insights into our daily lives involves both strategic planning and mindset adjustments. By setting flexible goals, seeking continuous feedback, and remaining open to change, we can better navigate the complexities of modern life. Additionally, practical tools such as scenario planning and stress management means provide concrete ways to prepare for and manage uncertainty. With these approaches in mind, we can approach uncertainty not as a paralyzing force but as a powerful catalyst for growth. As we delve into specifics, remember that the journey to mastering uncertainty is ongoing. It requires practice, patience, and a willingness to embrace the unknown as a vital part of the human experience.

The first step in dealing with uncertainty is adopting a growth mindset. This perspective encourages a renewed love for learning, which are crucial when facing the unknown. By viewing challenges as opportunities for growth rather than threats, you can maintain a positive outlook and stay motivated. Next time you encounter an unexpected challenge, remind yourself that this is an opportunity to grow. Reflect on past experiences where you overcame obstacles and learned something valuable. This will help reinforce the belief that you can handle new uncertainties with the same toughness. While routines can provide a sense of stability, it's important to incorporate flexibility into your daily schedule. A rigid routine can become a source of stress when disruptions occur. Instead, design a routine that allows for adjustments. This balance helps you stay grounded while remaining adaptable. Create a daily schedule that includes buffer times between tasks. These buffers allow you to handle unexpected events without feeling overwhelmed. For example, if you plan to work on a project from 9 am to 11 am, allocate 15 minutes at the end for any unforeseen delays. In the face of uncertainty, it's easy to become overwhelmed by factors beyond your control. To counter this, concentrate on what you can control. This approach not only reduces stress but also empowers you to take meaningful actions. Make a list of aspects within your control and those outside of it. For instance, you can control your effort, attitude, and response to situations. Focus on these elements, and let go of the rest. This shift in focus can significantly reduce anxiety and increase your sense of agency. Effective coping mechanisms are essential for managing stress and uncertainty. These mechanisms can include mental practices, physical exercise, and creative outlets. Mindfulness, in particular, has been shown to reduce stress by promoting present-moment awareness. Incorporate these methods, such as meditation or deep breathing exercises into your daily routine. Even just five minutes a day can make a difference. Additionally, find a physical activity you enjoy, whether it's jogging, yoga, or dancing, to help release built-up tension. Self-compassion involves treating yourself with the same kindness and understanding that you would offer a friend. It's about recognizing that setbacks and difficulties are part of the human experience. By being gentle with yourself, you can build yourself up. Practice self-compassion by acknowledging your struggles without judgment. When faced with a setback, instead of criticizing yourself, try saying, "This is tough, but I'm doing my best." This approach fosters self-love and helps you bounce back more quickly from adversity. Setting realistic, achievable goals provides a sense of direction and purpose, which can be particularly grounding during uncertain times. Break down large goals into smaller, manageable steps to maintain momentum and reduce overwhelm. Use the SMART criteria (Specific, Measurable, Achievable, Relevant, Time-bound) to set your goals. For example, instead of saying, "I want to get fit," set a specific goal like, "I will jog for 30 minutes three times a week for the next month." While staying informed is important, excessive consumption of news and social media can exacerbate anxiety. It's crucial to find a balance that keeps you aware without overwhelming you with information. Set specific times of the day to check the news and limit your exposure to potentially distressing information. For instance, you might choose to read the news for 30 minutes in the morning and then avoid checking it again until the evening. Having a strong support network is invaluable when dealing with uncertainty. Friends, family, and mentors can provide emotional support, practical advice, and different perspectives on your challenges. Regularly reach out to your support network, even when things are going well. Building and maintaining these relationships ensures that you have a reliable source of support when times get tough. Additionally, consider joining communities or groups with shared interests or goals. Gratitude can shift your focus from what you lack to what you have, fostering a positive outlook even in uncertain times. Regularly practicing gratitude can improve your emotional well-being. Keep a gratitude journal where you write down three things you're grateful for each day. These can be as simple as a delicious meal or a kind gesture from a friend. Reflecting on these moments can help you stay positive and grounded. Being prepared for various potential outcomes can reduce the fear of the unknown. By planning for different scenarios, you can feel more confident in your ability to handle whatever comes your way. Use a technique called scenario planning. Identify key uncertainties you face and develop plans for different possible outcomes. For example, if you're uncertain about a job opportunity, plan for scenarios where you get the job, don't get the job, or get a different offer.

Remember, the goal isn't to eliminate uncertainty but to develop the strength to thrive despite it. In our quest to handle uncertainty, one powerful approach is to harness the principles outlined in James Clear's "Atomic Habits." Clear's framework emphasizes the importance of small, incremental changes that compound over time to produce significant results. These habits not only provide a sense of stability but also create a foundation that helps us better navigate the unpredictable nature of modern life. Here, we'll explore how some of the core concepts from "Atomic Habits" can be applied to enhance our adaptability. Clear's central thesis is that **small, consistent actions** lead to remarkable results. This concept is particularly relevant when dealing with uncertainty. By focusing on tiny changes, we can gradually build it without overwhelming ourselves. Instead of trying to overhaul our lives in response to uncertainty, we make minor adjustments that, over time, significantly enhance our ability to cope. Start by identifying one small habit that can help manage uncertainty. For instance, if the uncertainty of your schedule causes stress, begin with a simple habit of reviewing your plan for the next day each evening. This small step can create a sense of preparedness and control. One effective technique from "Atomic Habits" is **habit stacking**, which involves linking a new habit to an existing one. This method leverages our current routines to introduce new behaviors more seamlessly. In the context of handling uncertainty, habit stacking can help us build routines without adding additional stress. If you already have a morning coffee routine, stack a new habit onto it. For example, while waiting for your coffee to brew, spend five minutes practicing mindfulness or setting your intentions for the day. This small addition can anchor your day in a positive mindset, making it easier to handle unforeseen challenges. Clear emphasizes the **importance of identity** in habit formation. By focusing on who we want to become, rather than what we want to achieve, we align our actions with our core values and long-term vision. When faced with uncertainty, maintaining a strong sense of identity can help us stay grounded and resilient. Rather than setting a vague goal like "handle uncertainty better," frame it in terms of your identity. For example, "I am a resilient person who embraces change." This identity-focused approach reinforces your commitment to it and makes it easier to adopt behaviors that align with this self-image. The **two-minute rule** suggests that when starting a new habit, it should take less than two minutes to complete. This makes the habit easy to start and reduces resistance. Applying this rule to uncertainty management can help build consistency without overwhelming effort. If you want to start journaling to process thoughts during uncertain times, begin with a two-minute journaling session each day. This minimal commitment lowers the barrier to entry and helps establish the habit. Over time, you can gradually extend the duration as it becomes a more ingrained part of your routine. Clear outlines **four laws of behavior change** that can be instrumental in handling uncertainty: Make it obvious, make it attractive, make it easy, and make it satisfying. These principles guide how we can effectively build habits that support it. Ensure your new habit is clearly defined and cued by existing routines. For example, place a journal on your bedside table as a reminder to write each night. Link new habits to positive experiences or rewards. Pair your habit of reading about stress management with enjoying a favorite snack. Simplify the habit to its core elements to reduce friction. Start with reading one page of a self-help book each day instead of committing to an entire chapter. Build in immediate rewards to reinforce the habit. After completing your daily mindfulness practice, reward yourself with a few minutes of a favorite activity. Clear also highlights the impact of our environment on habit formation. By designing our environment to support our desired habits, we can make it easier to manage uncertainty. Create a workspace that minimizes distractions and promotes focus. This might involve decluttering your desk, using noise-canceling headphones, or setting specific times for checking emails. An environment designed to reduce stress can help you stay calm and focused, even when faced with unpredictable challenges. Integrating these principles into your daily life involves consistency and reflection. Start with small, manageable changes and gradually build on them. Regularly reflect on your progress and adjust as needed. The goal is to create a resilient foundation that enables you to handle uncertainty with confidence and grace. Imagine you're preparing for a big presentation at work. Uncertainty about the outcome can cause anxiety. Applying Clear's principles, you could: schedule daily practice sessions and set reminders. Pair practice with listening to your favorite music afterward. Start with just five minutes of practice. Reward yourself with a small treat after each practice session. By consistently applying these small, incremental changes, you gradually build confidence and reduce anxiety about the presentation. This process not only prepares you for the immediate challenge but also enhances your overall ability to manage future uncertainties. Incorporating the principles from "Atomic Habits" into your approach to handling uncertainty can create a robust framework. These small, manageable changes compound over time, empowering you to face life's unpredictability with greater confidence and adaptability.

Handling uncertainty isn't just about theory; by adopting specific approaches, we can transform it from a daunting challenge into an opportunity for growth. One effective method for managing uncertainty is to implement a **daily reflection ritual**. Taking a few minutes each evening to reflect on your day can help you process experiences, learn from them, and plan for the next day. This ritual creates a sense of closure and preparation, fostering a mindset ready to tackle whatever comes next. Imagine this: at the end of each day, you spend five quiet minutes with a journal. You jot down three things you did well and one area where you could improve. This practice not only helps you see your progress but also instills a habit of continuous improvement. Over time, these small reflections accumulate, giving you insights into your patterns and helping you better handle uncertainty with a proactive mindset. **Visualization** is another powerful tool. Athletes and successful professionals often use it to prepare for uncertain situations. By mentally rehearsing potential scenarios, you can reduce anxiety and increase your readiness for various outcomes. Picture yourself before a significant event, such as a job interview or a public presentation. Spend ten minutes visualizing different scenarios. See yourself handling unexpected questions or technical issues with calm and competence. This inner rehearsal primes your mind to stay composed and focused, reducing the fear of the unknown. **Scenario planning** is all about preparing for multiple possible futures. This technique can help you feel more in control and ready to adapt to different outcomes. It's like having a backup plan for your backup plan, ensuring you're not caught off guard by sudden changes. For example, if you're managing a major project at work, sit down and brainstorm potential obstacles. What if a key team member leaves? What if your budget gets cut? Develop strategies for these scenarios in advance. This proactive approach not only mitigates the impact of unforeseen changes but also enhances your confidence in handling whatever comes your way. Setting **flexible goals** is another key strategy. Adaptive goals allow you to remain focused without becoming rigid. When circumstances change, your goals can adjust accordingly, keeping you on track even when the path shifts. Instead of setting a fixed goal like "I will complete this project in three months," frame it with flexibility: "I will aim to complete the first phase of the project in six weeks, but if obstacles arise, I will adjust the timeline accordingly." This approach keeps you motivated and adaptable, helping you stay productive without the stress of rigid deadlines. Creating a **personal mental toolkit** involves identifying and compiling resources that help you cope with stress and uncertainty. Think of it as your go-to collection of tools for tough times. Assemble a digital or physical toolkit. Include stress-relief methods like deep-breathing exercises, inspirational quotes, a list of supportive contacts, and quick access to mindfulness apps. Having these resources readily available ensures you have practical tools at your fingertips during challenging times, making it easier to bounce back from setbacks. Staying connected with your **support network** through regular check-ins provides emotional support and practical advice. These interactions remind you that you're not alone in facing uncertainty. Schedule bi-weekly coffee chats with a trusted friend or mentor. Use these check-ins to discuss your current challenges and brainstorm potential solutions. These conversations can provide new perspectives and reinforce your sense of community. **Gratitude** shifts your focus from what you lack to what you have, fostering a positive outlook even in uncertain times. Regularly practicing gratitude can improve your psychical well-being. Keep a gratitude journal where you write down three things you're grateful for each day. These can be as simple as a delicious meal or a kind gesture from a friend. Reflecting on these moments can help you stay positive and grounded, even when uncertainty looms large.

Consider Nicola, a marketing professional facing potential layoff at her company. To handle this uncertainty, she implements several practical approaches: Each night, Nicola reflects on her achievements and areas for growth, helping her stay positive and focused on her professional development. She visualizes herself thriving in different job scenarios, including freelancing and moving to a new industry, which boosts her confidence and readiness for change. Sarah creates a plan for various career outcomes, updating her resume, networking with industry contacts, and exploring new skills through online courses. To stay centered, she starts her mornings with a ten-minute meditation, fostering a sense of calm that carries through her day. She sets flexible career goals, such as "I will apply to at least five new job opportunities each week but will adapt based on the job market's response." By integrating these practices, she is better equipped to manage her career uncertainty with confidence. Incorporating these practical examples and applications into your routine can help you navigate the complexities of modern life with greater. Remember, the goal is not to eliminate uncertainty but to build the strength and flexibility to thrive despite it.

As we delve into the schemes for developing next-level equilibrium, it's essential to understand the personal journey that led me to this point. My career as a performance expert has spanned over two decades, encompassing work with military personnel, professional athletes, and corporate executives. However, the seeds of my approach were sown much earlier, rooted in my own life experiences and challenges. Growing up in a small town, I was no stranger to adversity. My family faced numerous financial and personal struggles, which taught me the importance of resilience from a young age. These early experiences instilled a drive to understand what makes some people crumble under pressure while others thrive. This curiosity led me to pursue a career where I could explore and teach the principles of willpower and peak performance. One of the pivotal moments in my career came when I began consulting for the military. The demands of military life—intense training, high-stakes missions, and the constant presence of danger—required a level of inner fortitude that was both inspiring and daunting. My role was to develop training programs that would help soldiers manage stress, stay focused, and perform under extreme pressure. This experience was transformative, providing deep insights into the human psyche and the incredible capacity for endurance and adaptability. Transitioning from military consulting to working with professional athletes was another significant chapter in my career. Athletes, much like soldiers, operate in high-pressure environments where the stakes are incredibly high. My work involved not only enhancing their physical performance but also building their inner balance. I developed personalized coaching methods that integrated mindfulness, stress management, and cognitive-behavioral strategies. One athlete, in particular, stands out in my memory. A world-class tennis player, he struggled with the rational aspect of the game. Despite his physical prowess, he often found himself losing crucial matches due to cognitive blocks and performance anxiety. Through our work together, we implemented a regimen that combined visualization techniques and adaptive goal setting. Over time, these approaches helped him not only improve his game but also gain a new sense of confidence and control, ultimately leading him to several major victories. My journey then led me to the corporate world, where I applied these to executive leadership and team development. High-level executives face a unique set of challenges, including relentless pressure, critical decision-making, and the need to inspire and lead others. My role was to help these leaders develop the inner fortitude necessary to navigate their complex environments effectively. In one memorable instance, I worked with a CEO of a major tech company undergoing a significant merger. The stress and uncertainty of the transition were palpable, affecting not only the executive team but the entire organization. By incorporating brain training into their routine, including stress management and strategic scenario planning, we were able to steer the company through the turbulence successfully. This experience reinforced the universal applicability of these principles across different fields and industries. While my professional experiences were invaluable, my personal life also presented significant challenges that shaped my understanding of the world. A defining moment came when I faced a severe health scare. The uncertainty and fear during that period tested my inner fortitude in ways I had never anticipated. Applying the very strategies I had been teaching I navigated through this difficult time, emerging stronger and more committed to my mission. My passion for endurance sports, such as marathons and triathlons, has been a personal laboratory for testing all that you now see in this book. The grueling training and the physical and psychical demands of these sports have taught me invaluable lessons about pushing limits, embracing discomfort, and the power of perseverance. These diverse experiences—from the battlefield to the boardroom, from personal health battles to the endurance track—have all contributed to the development of the "Warrior Mindset 2.0." This approach is not just theoretical; it is grounded in real-world applications and personal triumphs. The principles you will encounter in this book are the culmination of a lifetime of learning, teaching, and living the principles. As we move forward, I will share more about how these experiences have shaped the specific ways outlined in this book. My hope is that by understanding the journey behind these methods, you will find them even more relevant and powerful in your own quest for reaching our highest potential.

Recovery and Regeneration

In the relentless pursuit of peak performance, the concept of recovery often takes a backseat. However, recovery is not merely a passive state but an active and crucial component of achieving sustained high performance. Without adequate recovery, the body and mind cannot function at their optimal levels, leading to burnout, injury, and diminished returns on effort. The importance of recovery in achieving peak performance cannot be overstated. Athletes, executives, and high achievers across various fields have long recognized that without proper rest and regeneration, their ability to perform consistently at the highest levels is compromised. Recovery allows the body to repair tissues, replenish energy stores, and reduce fatigue. For the mind, it means processing information, consolidating memories, and maintaining emotional balance. In essence, recovery is the foundation upon which sustained performance is built. Modern recovery techniques have evolved significantly, informed by advancements in science and technology. Traditional methods like sleep and nutrition remain vital, but they are now complemented by a host of innovative approaches designed to enhance and expedite the recovery process.

Physical recovery begins at the cellular level, where the body undertakes the critical process of repairing and rebuilding muscle fibers. During intense physical activity, muscle fibers undergo microscopic tears. This muscle damage is not harmful; rather, it is the catalyst for muscle growth and increased strength. The repair process is facilitated by satellite cells, a type of stem cell located on the periphery of muscle fibers. When activated by muscle damage, satellite cells proliferate and fuse with the damaged fibers, donating their nuclei to help repair the tear. Protein synthesis is a vital part of this repair process. Following exercise, the body increases protein synthesis rates to rebuild damaged muscle fibers stronger than before, a phenomenon known as muscle hypertrophy. This process is heavily influenced by nutritional intake, particularly the consumption of protein and amino acids, which provide the necessary building blocks for new muscle tissue. Additionally, mechanical tension, muscle damage, and metabolic stress from exercise stimulate anabolic signaling pathways, such as the mTOR pathway, which further promotes protein synthesis and muscle growth. Inflammation is the body's natural response to muscle damage and is essential for initiating the healing process. Acute inflammation involves the release of signaling molecules called cytokines, which attract immune cells to the site of muscle damage. These immune cells, including macrophages, play a crucial role in clearing out damaged cells and debris, setting the stage for tissue repair and regeneration. However, while acute inflammation is beneficial, chronic inflammation can be detrimental, leading to prolonged recovery times and potential injury. Therefore, managing inflammation through appropriate recovery is critical. Balancing inflammation involves using methods such as cold therapy to reduce excessive swelling and incorporating anti-inflammatory foods, like those rich in omega-3 fatty acids, into the diet to help modulate the immune response. During exercise, the body's primary energy source, glycogen, is rapidly depleted. Glycogen, stored in muscles and the liver, is broken down into glucose, fueling muscle contractions and sustaining physical activity. As exercise continues, ATP (adenosine triphosphate) stores, the immediate source of energy, are also utilized. Once these stores are exhausted, the body enters a catabolic state where muscle protein is broken down to produce glucose, leading to muscle fatigue and decreased performance. To effectively replenish these energy stores, consuming carbohydrates post-exercise is essential. Carbohydrates are broken down into glucose, which is then stored as glycogen in the muscles and liver. The timing of carbohydrate intake is crucial; consuming carbs within 30 minutes to 2 hours post-exercise can significantly enhance glycogen resynthesis. Pairing carbohydrates with protein in a 3:1 ratio can further boost glycogen storage and muscle repair. For example, a recovery meal might include a banana with peanut butter or a protein shake with fruit. Nutrient timing extends beyond immediate post-exercise intake. Consistent fueling throughout the day supports metabolic recovery by maintaining stable blood glucose levels and providing a continuous supply of nutrients for muscle repair and energy replenishment. Complex carbohydrates, lean proteins, and healthy fats should be included in regular meals and snacks to sustain energy levels and promote recovery. Hydration is also critical, as adequate fluid intake helps transport nutrients to cells and supports metabolic processes. Exercise induces significant hormonal changes, which are crucial for adaptation and recovery. Cortisol, known as the stress hormone, increases during intense exercise to mobilize energy by breaking down glycogen, fat, and protein. While beneficial in the short term, chronic elevation of cortisol can impair recovery and lead to muscle breakdown. Conversely, anabolic hormones like testosterone and growth hormone, which promote muscle repair and growth, may initially decrease post-exercise but are crucial for long-term recovery. Sleep is vital for hormonal regulation. During deep sleep, the body releases growth hormone, which stimulates tissue repair and muscle growth. Aim for 7-9 hours of quality sleep per night, with a focus on maintaining a consistent sleep schedule. Chronic stress can elevate cortisol levels, hindering recovery. Incorporating stress management techniques such as mindfulness, meditation, and deep-breathing exercises can help maintain cortisol levels within a healthy range. Consuming a balanced diet rich in vitamins and minerals supports hormone production and regulation. Foods high in omega-3 fatty acids, like salmon and flaxseeds, can reduce inflammation and cortisol levels, while protein-rich foods support the production of anabolic hormones. Understanding the natural fluctuations of hormonal cycles can also aid in optimizing recovery. For instance, training intensity can be adjusted according to circadian rhythms, which influence hormone levels. High-intensity training might be more effective when testosterone levels are naturally higher, typically in the late morning. Conversely, lower-intensity activities or recovery sessions might be scheduled during times of higher cortisol, such as late afternoon, to balance hormonal effects and enhance recovery. The nervous system, encompassing both the central (CNS) and peripheral (PNS) nervous systems, is integral to coordinating and executing physical activities. Intense or prolonged exercise can lead to nervous system fatigue, which affects overall performance and recovery. CNS fatigue manifests as mental exhaustion, reduced motivation, and impaired cognitive function, while PNS fatigue involves diminished motor function and muscle responsiveness. Sleep is crucial for CNS recovery, as it allows the brain to process information, consolidate memories, and repair neural pathways. Prioritizing sleep hygiene practices, such as maintaining a regular sleep schedule and creating a restful sleep environment, can enhance recovery. Low-intensity activities, such as light jogging, swimming, or yoga, can maintain blood flow and support neural recovery without causing additional fatigue. These activities help reduce muscle stiffness and promote relaxation, aiding in the recovery of both the CNS and PNS. Incorporating relaxation practices, such as deep breathing, meditation, and progressive muscle relaxation, can reduce emotional stress and promote recovery of the CNS. These systems help lower cortisol levels, improve mood, and enhance overall well-being. Training the nervous system to become more resilient can also improve recovery. Some, such as neurofeedback, which involves training individuals to regulate their brain wave activity, can enhance cognitive function and reduce mental fatigue. Additionally, balancing intense training sessions with adequate recovery periods prevents overtraining and supports long-term nervous system health.

Mental fatigue is a state of tiredness that occurs when the brain is overworked. Unlike physical fatigue, which manifests as muscle tiredness, it affects cognitive functions such as decision-making, attention, and memory. Prolonged periods of intense psychological activity can deplete neurotransmitters, reduce neural efficiency, and lead to decreased brain performance. This fatigue is a result of continuous cognitive demands placed on the brain without adequate periods of rest and recovery. Emotional well-being is integral to overall psychical health and performance. Emotions influence motivation, focus, and decision-making processes. Negative emotional states, such as stress, anxiety, and depression, can impair cognitive functions, leading to reduced productivity and performance. Positive emotional states, on the other hand, enhance cognitive abilities, foster creativity, and improve problem-solving skills. Maintaining emotional balance is thus essential for sustained high performance. Neuroplasticity allows the brain to form new neural connections in response to learning and experience. However, for neuroplasticity to occur effectively, the brain requires periods of rest. During these rest periods, the brain consolidates information, strengthens neural connections, and repairs any damage caused by stress or intense cognitive activity. Without sufficient rest, the brain's ability to adapt and learn is compromised. Neurotransmitters are chemical messengers that transmit signals across synapses in the brain. They play a crucial role in regulating mood, cognition, and overall brain function. Continuous mental exertion can deplete levels of key neurotransmitters such as dopamine, serotonin, and norepinephrine. This depletion can lead to symptoms of mental fatigue, decreased motivation, and impaired cognitive performance. Recovery periods allow for the replenishment of these neurotransmitters, restoring optimal brain function. Cognitive Load

Theory posits that the brain has a limited capacity for processing information at any given time. When cognitive load exceeds this capacity, performance deteriorates, leading to errors and decreased efficiency. Emotional recovery is necessary to reduce cognitive load and prevent cognitive overload. Methods such as taking breaks, engaging in leisure activities, and practicing self-awareness can help manage cognitive load and enhance cognitive performance. Effective stress management is crucial for maintaining mental and emotional health. Chronic stress can lead to the release of cortisol, a hormone that, in high levels, can damage brain cells, particularly in areas involved in memory and learning such as the hippocampus. Deep breathing activates the parasympathetic nervous system, which counteracts the stress response and promotes relaxation. Systems such as diaphragmatic breathing and the 4-7-8 breathing method can be effective in reducing stress. Progressive muscle relaxation involves tensing and then slowly relaxing each muscle group in the body. It helps reduce physical tension and promotes a state of relaxation, aiding in stress reduction. Regular exercise has been shown to reduce levels of stress hormones and increase the production of endorphins, chemicals in the brain that act as natural painkillers and mood elevators. Organizing tasks and managing time effectively can reduce the cognitive load and prevent the feeling of being overwhelmed, which is a common cause of stress. Cognitive-behavioral techniques (CBT) are effective in addressing negative thought patterns and emotional responses. CBT helps individuals recognize and change distorted thinking, which can lead to improved emotional well-being and reduced stress. Techniques include cognitive restructuring, where negative thoughts are identified and challenged, and behavioral activation, which encourages engagement in enjoyable and meaningful activities to improve mood. Social support is a key factor in emotional recovery. Positive social interactions and strong relationships provide emotional comfort, reduce stress, and enhance one's overall well-being. Engaging with family, friends, or support groups can provide a sense of belonging and reduce feelings of isolation. Sharing experiences and seeking advice can also provide new perspectives and coping strategies for managing stress and emotional challenges. Rest and leisure activities play a vital role in emotional recovery. Engaging in hobbies and activities that one enjoys can provide a mental break from daily stressors and promote relaxation. Leisure activities, such as reading, gardening, or playing a musical instrument, can enhance mood, stimulate the brain, and provide a sense of accomplishment. Ensuring regular periods of rest and engaging in pleasurable activities can help maintain emotional balance and improve overall well-being. Dedicate 10-15 minutes each day to meditation. This can be done through guided sessions, apps, or simply sitting quietly and focusing on the breath. Incorporate regular breaks into work or study sessions. Develop a routine that includes stress management techniques such as deep breathing, progressive muscle relaxation, or physical activity. This can be tailored to individual preferences and schedules. Make time for social activities and interactions. This could involve regular meetups with friends, participating in group activities, or engaging in online communities.

Allocate time each week for leisure activities that are enjoyable and relaxing. This could involve hobbies, creative pursuits, or simply spending time in nature.

As we delve deeper into the science of recovery, it becomes evident that a comprehensive approach to rest and regeneration is not a luxury but a necessity for anyone aiming to excel in their field. Recent advancements in recovery science have provided us with a deeper understanding of how the body and mind recuperate and the critical role recovery plays in achieving peak performance. Together we will explore the latest research in recovery science and discuss key findings and their implications for performance. Recent research in the science of recovery has yielded groundbreaking insights that are reshaping how athletes and high performers approach rest and regeneration. One of the most significant areas of focus is the role of genetic factors in recovery. A study published in *Nature Communications* highlighted that certain genetic markers can predict an individual's response to different recovery approaches, suggesting a future where recovery protocols are tailored to one's genetic profile. Another innovative area of research is the use of artificial intelligence (AI) to optimize recovery routines. AI algorithms analyze data from wearable devices, such as sleep patterns, heart rate variability (HRV), and activity levels, to provide personalized recovery recommendations in real-time. The role of gut health in recovery has come to the forefront. Studies from the *American Journal of Physiology* have shown that a healthy gut microbiome can significantly influence inflammation and immune responses, which are critical to the recovery process. Researchers are now exploring probiotics and dietary interventions as means to enhance gut health and, consequently, recovery efficiency. Cryotherapy and its benefits have also been validated by recent studies. Research published in the *Journal of Sports Sciences* has demonstrated that whole-body cryotherapy can reduce muscle soreness and inflammation more effectively than traditional ice baths. This method involves short exposures to extremely cold temperatures and is becoming increasingly popular among elite athletes. Lastly, advancements in neurofeedback technology are providing new ways to enhance cerebral recovery. Studies from the *Journal of Neurotherapy* indicate that neurofeedback, which trains individuals to regulate brain wave activity, can improve cognitive function and reduce mental fatigue. This technique is particularly useful for high performers who need to maintain sharp intellectual acuity under stress. These cutting-edge research findings underscore the dynamic nature of recovery science, offering exciting possibilities for more effective and personalized recovery strategies.

Sleep has long been recognized as a fundamental component of recovery, but recent studies have shed light on its multifaceted role in performance enhancement. Research conducted by the Sleep Research Society has highlighted the significance of sleep stages, particularly deep sleep (slow-wave sleep) and REM (rapid eye movement) sleep, in physical and cognitive recovery. Deep sleep is essential for bodily recovery, as it is during this stage that the body releases growth hormones necessary for tissue repair and muscle growth. REM sleep, on the other hand, is crucial for cognitive functions, such as memory consolidation and emotional regulation. **Nutritional science** has made considerable strides in understanding how the timing of nutrient intake affects recovery. Studies published in the Journal of the International Society of Sports Nutrition emphasize the importance of consuming protein and carbohydrates within the post-exercise window (typically within 30 minutes to 2 hours after exercise) to maximize muscle glycogen resynthesis and repair. The research underscores that the quality and timing of nutrient intake can significantly influence recovery speed and efficiency. **Active recovery**, which involves engaging in low-intensity activities post-exercise, has been the focus of several recent studies. Research from the American College of Sports Medicine indicates that active recovery helps to maintain blood flow, which aids in the removal of metabolic waste products like lactic acid. Ways such as yoga, stretching, and light aerobic exercises have been shown to reduce muscle soreness and improve flexibility, contributing to faster recovery times and enhanced performance in subsequent training sessions. The importance of **emotional recovery** has gained increasing recognition. Research from the Mindfulness Research and Practice initiative at the University of Oxford has demonstrated that these practices can significantly reduce stress and enhance cognitive clarity. These practices help to manage the psychological load associated with high-performance environments, ensuring that mental fatigue does not impair decision-making and focus. **Wearable technology** has revolutionized the way we monitor and enhance recovery. Devices that track heart rate variability (HRV) provide valuable insights into the autonomic nervous system's status, offering a clear picture of the body's readiness to perform. Studies in the Journal of Sports Sciences have shown that higher HRV is associated with better recovery and a greater capacity for physical exertion. Compression garments and devices like pneumatic compression boots have also been validated by research, such as studies from the National Institutes of Health, for their effectiveness in reducing muscle soreness and improving circulation, thereby speeding up the recovery process.

After the initial phase of his recovery, which focused on stabilizing his corporeal condition and addressing immediate medical needs, Michael Radcliffe embarked on a journey that required immense psychical and physical strength. This second stage of recovery was characterized by innovative and unorthodox methods that challenged conventional approaches and pushed the boundaries of what was considered possible. I vividly remember the turning point in Michael's recovery journey. It was a crisp autumn morning when we decided to take a different approach to his rehabilitation. The traditional methods had helped, but we both felt that something more was needed to truly reignite his spirit and accelerate his progress. Inspired by our childhood love for adventure, we decided to incorporate elements of adaptive therapy into his recovery plan. We began with accessible nature excursions, gradually increasing their complexity as Michael's strength and confidence grew. These excursions were not just about physical exercise; they were about reconnecting with the environment, grounding oneself, and finding peace amidst the chaos. Research has shown that spending time in nature can significantly reduce stress and improve cognitive clarity. For Michael, these excursions became a meditative practice, helping him process the emotional trauma of his accident and find a sense of calm and purpose. One memorable experience was a weekend stay at an accessible cabin in the mountains. Away from the distractions of daily life, Michael found solace in the serenity of nature. Each day, we would set small goals – reaching a particular lookout point using adaptive trails, identifying different species of plants from the pathways, or simply sitting by a stream and listening to the water. These activities not only strengthened his physical abilities but also provided a mental escape, allowing him to reflect and heal. In addition to outdoor therapy, we explored various holistic therapies. One technique that stood out was equine-assisted therapy, which involves interactions with horses to promote emotional growth and learning. Michael had always been fond of animals, and working with horses helped him develop trust, empathy, and patience. The gentle nature of the horses and the need for clear, calm communication mirrored the control and focus Michael needed in his recovery. Studies have shown that equine-assisted therapy can improve physical skills, reduce anxiety, and increase self-esteem, all of which were crucial for Michael's journey. Another unorthodox approach we embraced was the practice of adaptive yoga and seated Tai Chi. These practices focus on the mind-body connection, promoting flexibility, balance, and inner tranquility. For Michael, who was dealing with both physiological limitations and emotional scars, these practices were transformative. Adaptive yoga helped him regain his physical strength and flexibility, while seated Tai Chi's slow, deliberate movements and focus on breathing provided a form of moving meditation that enhanced his cerebral adaptability. The emphasis on mindfulness in both practices helped Michael stay present and focused, reducing his anxiety about the future and fostering a sense of inner peace. We also leveraged modern technology to support Michael's recovery. Virtual reality (VR) became an unexpected but powerful tool. VR allowed Michael to engage in immersive environments that simulated various fitness exercises and social interactions, all from the safety and comfort of home. These virtual experiences helped bridge the gap between his current capabilities and his aspirations, providing a safe space to practice and build confidence. For instance, VR sessions that simulated walking in a bustling city or exploring a forest enabled Michael to gradually confront and overcome his fears and limitations. Throughout this journey, the role of community and support networks cannot be overstated. We joined a local support group for individuals recovering from severe injuries, which provided a platform for sharing experiences, advice, and encouragement. This sense of belonging and mutual understanding was incredibly empowering for Michael. Being part of a community where others were facing similar challenges helped him feel less isolated and more hopeful about his recovery. It's clear that the combination of traditional methods with innovative and unorthodox techniques played a crucial role in his progress. The holistic approach, which included adaptive outdoor therapy, equine-assisted therapy, adaptive yoga, seated Tai Chi, and the use of VR, addressed both his physical and psychical needs, fostering a more comprehensive and effective recovery process. Michael's journey taught us that recovery is not just about healing the body but also nurturing the mind and spirit. It's about finding balance, embracing new experiences, and pushing the boundaries of what is possible. Through these efforts, Michael not only regained his strength but also rediscovered his zest for life, emerging stronger and more resilient than ever before.

Understanding that recovery needs change over time is crucial for maintaining long-term health and performance. Sustainable recovery practices require adaptability, personalization, and an ongoing commitment to self-awareness and education. During the stages of youth and early adulthood, recovery practices should focus on building robust habits that can sustain intense fitness exercises and emotional demands. Emphasize the importance of sleep, balanced nutrition, and foundational perception practices. Recent research from the *Journal of Adolescent Health* indicates that establishing strong recovery routines early in life can enhance long-term well-being and performance. As responsibilities increase with career and family, recovery practices need to adapt to accommodate higher stress levels and potentially less free time. Methods such as micro-recovery breaks and integrating family-friendly physical activities can be beneficial. The *American Journal of Preventive Medicine* highlights the importance of maintaining fitness and mental health practices during midlife to combat the increased risk of chronic stress and burnout. In later years, recovery should focus on maintaining mobility, cognitive function, and emotional well-being. Activities like low-impact exercise, advanced meditation practices, and social engagement become more critical. Studies in the *Journal of Aging and Health* show that tailored recovery practices for older adults can significantly improve quality of life and longevity.

Regularly assess your physical and psychical state using tools like wearable technology, journaling, or professional evaluations. Personalized data can guide the adjustment of recovery practices to meet current needs. Recovery plans should be flexible and adaptable. Integrate a variety of styles and be open to changing them based on feedback from your body and mind. Research from the *Journal of Sports Sciences* supports the effectiveness of personalized recovery strategies over standardized routines. Use insights from behavioral science to build sustainable recovery habits. Courses of action like habit stacking, where new recovery habits are linked to existing routines, can enhance consistency and effectiveness. The *Journal of Behavioral Medicine* notes that integrating recovery practices into daily habits can lead to more sustainable lifestyle changes. Set clear, achievable recovery goals and regularly review progress. Use feedback loops to refine and optimize the recovery. Studies from *Behavioral Science & Policy* suggest that goal-setting and regular feedback significantly improve adherence to health and wellness routines. Utilize the latest wearable technology to monitor a broader range of physiological metrics, including HRV, sleep stages, and stress levels. These devices provide real-time feedback and personalized recovery recommendations. Research from *Nature Digital Medicine* indicates that advanced wearables can enhance recovery by providing precise and actionable data. Leverage AI-driven platforms that analyze personal health data to predict recovery needs and suggest optimal practices. These systems can adapt recommendations based on ongoing data input, ensuring a continually optimized recovery plan. Studies in *Artificial Intelligence in Medicine* highlight the potential of AI in personalizing health interventions. Keep abreast of the latest research in recovery science and behavioral health. Engaging with current literature and attending workshops or webinars can provide new insights. Join communities and support groups that focus on recovery and well-being. Sharing experiences and learning from others can provide motivation and new perspectives. Practice regular self-reflection to assess the effectiveness of your recovery practices. Mindfulness and journaling can help identify what works best and what needs adjustment. Recognize the importance of mental health in the recovery process. Seek professional support when needed and prioritize practices that support emotional well-being alongside physical recovery. Ensure that your recovery plan addresses physical, psychical, and emotional needs. Integrate a variety of ways that complement each other, providing comprehensive support. Focus on building sustainable habits that can be maintained over the long term. Small, consistent practices often have a more significant impact than sporadic, intense efforts. Strive for a balance between professional responsibilities and personal recovery needs. Incorporate recovery practices into your daily routine in a way that supports both work and personal life. Maintain a flexible mindset that allows for adjustments as life circumstances change. Being adaptable ensures that your recovery practices remain effective and relevant over time.

As we wrap up this chapter on integrating recovery into daily life, it's clear that the path to sustained peak performance lies in more than just hard work—it's about smart recovery. Remember, recovery is not a passive act but an active, intentional process that requires your attention and dedication. Embrace the concept of evolving recovery practices that grow with you through different stages of life. Whether you're at the peak of your career, balancing family responsibilities, or enjoying the later stages of life, your recovery needs will change, and your approach should adapt accordingly. Tailoring your recovery plan is essential. Use advanced technologies, such as wearable devices and AI-driven platforms, to gain insights into your unique recovery needs. Stay informed about the latest research and continuously seek ways to optimize your recovery practices. The better you understand your body and mind, the more effectively you can respond to their needs. Let's not forget the importance of community and support networks. Engaging with others who share similar goals and challenges can provide motivation, new perspectives, and emotional support. Surround yourself with people who encourage your growth. Ultimately, creating a balanced approach to recovery is about integrating these practices seamlessly into your daily routine. Make recovery a habit, not an afterthought. Celebrate the small victories and learn from every setback. By committing to a comprehensive and adaptive recovery strategy, you're not only enhancing your performance but also ensuring long-term well-being. Embrace this journey with the knowledge that every rest period, every mindful moment, and every act of self-care is a step toward becoming a stronger, more resilient version of yourself. Let recovery be your secret weapon in the pursuit of excellence.

Advanced Emotional Resilience

In today's ever-changing world, emotional resilience stands as a crucial skill that can determine our ability to thrive amidst challenges. We are referring to the capacity to navigate through life's ups and downs with a stable and positive mindset, bouncing back from adversity stronger and wiser. This skill is not about avoiding difficulties but rather facing them head-on and emerging resilient, adaptable, and ready for what's next. In the modern world, we are constantly bombarded with stressors—whether it's the pressures of work, the relentless news cycle, or personal challenges. The ability to maintain emotional stability in the face of these stressors is more critical than ever. It helps us manage our reactions, maintain perspective, and stay grounded even when the world around us feels chaotic. It's the difference between being overwhelmed by emotions and using them as fuel for growth and performance. This chapter delves into advanced strategies for managing emotions in the modern world, offering unique techniques that you can apply to enhance your emotional toughness. We'll explore the underlying triggers that set off emotional responses and provide practical methods for regulating these reactions. By understanding and managing our emotions, we can improve our cognitive performance and overall well-being. We will begin by identifying common emotional triggers and learning how to recognize them in our daily lives. From there, we'll move on to discuss various methods for emotional regulation, drawing on both my personal experiences and recent psychological research. These means include mindfulness practices, cognitive restructuring, and other practical ones designed to help you regain control over your emotional landscape.

Emotional intelligence involves understanding and managing your own emotions while also being attuned to the emotions of others. Enhancing this skill can also improve interpersonal relationships and professional success. Building a support system is another vital aspect. We'll cover the importance of having a network of supportive relationships and offer tips on how to cultivate and maintain these connections. Personal anecdotes from my own journey and my brother's experiences will illustrate the profound impact a strong support system can have. Finally, we'll provide practical applications and exercises that you can integrate into your daily life. These activities are designed to strengthen your emotional resilience gradually, helping you to become more adaptable and emotionally stable over time. By the end of this chapter, you will have a comprehensive toolkit for managing your emotions and maintaining flexibility in the face of modern challenges. In summary, this is not a static trait but a dynamic skill that can be developed and refined. With the right mindset, you can transform your emotional responses into a source of strength. Let's embark on this journey to master this tool and unlock your potential for sustained performance and well-being.

In our hyperconnected and rapidly changing world, emotional triggers are abundant. These triggers are stimuli that provoke strong emotional reactions, often overwhelming us with stress, anger, anxiety, or sadness. Recognizing and understanding these triggers is the first step toward developing advanced emotional skills. One of the most common emotional triggers is **work-related stress**. In the modern workplace, employees are often expected to juggle multiple tasks, meet tight deadlines, and continuously adapt to new technologies and processes. This constant pressure can lead to feelings of inadequacy and burnout. For instance, an unexpected criticism from a supervisor can trigger intense feelings of self-doubt and anxiety. **Financial instability** is another significant trigger. With economic uncertainty, many people experience stress related to job security, debt, and the cost of living. Worrying about finances can lead to chronic stress, affecting both psychical and physical health. **Social media and information overload** also play a significant role in triggering emotional responses. Constant exposure to curated images of others' seemingly perfect lives can evoke feelings of inadequacy and envy. Additionally, the barrage of news, often highlighting negative events, can lead to a sense of helplessness and fear. **Personal relationships** are a major source of emotional triggers. Misunderstandings, conflicts, and unmet expectations with family, friends, or partners can provoke intense emotional reactions. For example, a minor argument with a loved one can escalate into a significant emotional episode due to unresolved issues or miscommunications. I faced a profound emotional challenge when I received the news of my brother Michael's accident. The phone call came out of the blue, shattering my sense of normalcy and plunging me into a whirlwind of emotions. I recall the moment vividly—the ringing of the phone, the sinking feeling in my stomach as I heard the news, and the subsequent rush of fear, anger, and helplessness. My initial reaction was one of overwhelming panic. The uncertainty surrounding my brother's condition was a powerful emotional trigger, igniting a storm of anxiety and dread. As I rushed to the hospital, I found myself grappling with a flood of "what if" scenarios, each more distressing than the last. The situation forced me to confront my deepest fears and vulnerabilities, pushing me to the brink of emotional exhaustion. This experience highlighted the importance of understanding and managing emotional triggers. For me, the trigger was the sudden and unexpected news of my brother's accident. The intense emotional response it provoked was a natural reaction to a traumatic event. However, through this ordeal, I learned valuable lessons about identifying and coping with emotional triggers. Identifying and understanding one's emotional triggers is crucial for developing it. While we often discuss mindfulness and journaling, let's explore some different, yet equally effective schemes that can help you identify and understand your emotional triggers. Tracking your habits and behaviors over time can be an effective way to identify patterns in your emotional responses. Use a habit-tracking app or a simple spreadsheet to record daily activities, mood changes, and emotional reactions. Over time, you might notice that certain activities or times of day consistently trigger specific emotions. For instance, you may find that you feel particularly stressed after long meetings or anxious when you skip your morning routine. Pay attention to your physical and social environment and how it affects your emotions. Are there specific places, sounds, or smells that trigger strong emotional reactions? Sometimes, our surroundings can have a profound impact on our mood and emotional state. By becoming more aware of these environmental factors, you can start to identify and modify the aspects of your environment that contribute to emotional distress. Engaging in reflective dialogue with a trusted friend, family member, or therapist can provide deeper insights into your emotional triggers. Discussing your feelings and reactions with someone else can help you see patterns and triggers that you might not recognize on your own. This process of verbalizing your thoughts can lead to greater self-awareness and understanding. Biofeedback involves using electronic devices to monitor physiological functions like heart rate, muscle tension, and skin conductivity. By observing these physical indicators, you can gain insights into how your body reacts to stress and other emotional triggers. Over time, biofeedback can help you learn to recognize and control these physiological responses, leading to better emotional regulation. Visualization is a powerful tool for understanding emotional triggers. Take time to visualize past experiences that elicited strong emotional reactions. Try to remember the details: Where were you? Who was there? What was said or done? By revisiting these memories in a safe and controlled manner, you can start to identify common elements that act as triggers. This technique can also help you process and reframe these experiences, reducing their emotional impact over time. Engaging in creative activities like drawing, painting, or writing can help you explore and understand your emotions. Artistic expression allows you to externalize and examine your feelings in a tangible form. You might find that certain colors, themes, or symbols repeatedly appear in your work, indicating underlying emotional triggers. This method can be particularly effective for those who find verbal expression challenging. Expanding your emotional vocabulary can help you better identify and articulate your triggers. Often, we experience complex emotions that are difficult to describe with basic terms like "sad" or "angry." By learning more nuanced emotional terms, you can more accurately pinpoint your feelings and the situations that trigger them. This clarity can enhance your ability to manage and respond to emotional triggers effectively. Physical activity can be a powerful way to connect with and understand your emotions. Engaging in activities like yoga, dance, or martial arts helps you become more attuned to your body's signals. These practices encourage awareness of bodily sensations, which can reveal how physical states correlate with emotional triggers. For example, noticing tension in your shoulders might help you recognize when you are feeling stressed or anxious. These approaches will be able to empower you to navigate the complexities of modern life with greater ease and confidence.

Through my personal journey and professional experiences, I've discovered several practical techniques that have significantly helped me regulate my emotions. Here, I'll share these methods, provide personal stories that illustrate their effectiveness, and briefly reference recent psychological studies to support these approaches. As previously mentioned, consciousness has been a game-changer for me. It involves paying attention to the present moment without judgment, which helps in recognizing and accepting our emotions as they are. This practice allows us to create a space between our emotions and our reactions to them, providing clarity and calmness. I remember a particularly stressful period during my brother Michael's recovery. The uncertainty of his prognosis was overwhelming, and I often found myself spiraling into anxiety. I started practicing it by setting aside just ten minutes each day to sit quietly and focus on my breath. Initially, it was challenging to quiet my racing thoughts, but over time, I noticed a shift. I became more aware of my emotional triggers and less reactive to them. Research supports its benefits: a study published in the journal *Emotion* found that it can reduce emotional reactivity and improve emotional regulation. By practicing it, I've been able to approach stressful situations with a clearer mind and a more balanced emotional state. Deep breathing is another technique that has proven incredibly effective for me. It's simple, yet powerful. By taking slow, deep breaths, we can activate the body's relaxation response, which counteracts the stress response. During one of the most challenging moments of Michael's recovery, I found myself on the verge of a panic attack. My heart was racing, my palms were sweaty, and I felt an overwhelming sense of dread. Remembering the deep breathing exercises I had learned, I closed my eyes and took a slow, deep breath in through my nose, held it for a few seconds, and then exhaled slowly through my mouth. I repeated this several times. Gradually, I felt my heart rate slow down, and a sense of calm washed over me. The science behind deep breathing is well-documented. Research from Harvard Medical School indicates that deep breathing can reduce stress and promote relaxation by stimulating the parasympathetic nervous system. This simple practice has become a go-to technique for me whenever I feel overwhelmed. Cognitive restructuring involves identifying and challenging negative thought patterns that contribute to emotional distress. This technique has been particularly helpful for me in transforming my mindset and reactions. In the early days following Michael's accident, I was plagued by thoughts of "What if things never get better?" or "Why did this have to happen to us?" These thoughts were not only distressing but also unproductive. I decided to try cognitive restructuring by writing down these negative thoughts and then challenging them with evidence and alternative perspectives. For example, instead of thinking, "Things will never get better," I reframed it to, "We are doing everything we can, and there is hope for improvement each day." This technique has roots in cognitive-behavioral therapy (CBT), which has been extensively studied for its effectiveness in managing emotional disorders. A study in the *Journal of Consulting and Clinical Psychology* found that CBT, which includes cognitive restructuring, significantly reduces symptoms of anxiety and depression. By changing the way I think about challenges, I've been able to manage my emotions more effectively. Beyond these, personal experiences have underscored their importance. During Michael's rehabilitation, there were numerous setbacks. Each time, I relied on these methods to navigate the emotional turbulence. When Michael struggled with physical therapy, I used meditation to stay present and supportive. During nights filled with uncertainty, deep breathing helped me find calm. And cognitive restructuring allowed me to maintain hope and focus on positive outcomes, rather than getting lost in negative spirals.

One memorable instance was when Michael faced a particularly tough physical therapy session. He was frustrated and in pain, and I felt helpless watching him struggle. I suggested we take a few moments to breathe deeply together. As we breathed, I reminded him of the progress he had already made and reframed the session as a step towards recovery, rather than an insurmountable obstacle. This moment of shared awareness and cognitive restructuring not only calmed us both but also strengthened our resolve to keep pushing forward. Recent psychological studies provide further validation for these techniques. Mindfulness, as mentioned earlier, has been shown to reduce emotional reactivity. A study published in *Psychiatry Research* found that an eight-week mindfulness-based stress reduction program significantly decreased participants' levels of anxiety and depression. Deep breathing, or diaphragmatic breathing, has been supported by research in the *Journal of Evidence-Based Complementary & Alternative Medicine*. The study found that deep breathing exercises significantly reduced stress levels and improved emotional well-being in participants. Cognitive restructuring, a core component of CBT, has been extensively researched. A meta-analysis in the *Cognitive Therapy and Research* journal highlighted that CBT is highly effective in treating a range of emotional disorders, with cognitive restructuring playing a pivotal role in its success. By incorporating these methods into your daily routine, you can develop a more resilient and balanced emotional life.

Emotional intelligence (EI) is the ability to understand, manage, and effectively express one's own emotions, as well as to engage and navigate with others' emotions. Daniel Goleman, who popularized the concept, breaks it down into five key components: self-awareness, self-regulation, motivation, empathy, and social skills. These elements collectively contribute to our ability to handle stress, communicate effectively, and overcome challenges. Recent research on emotional intelligence (EI) has significantly advanced our understanding of its impact on overall well-being. One of the key findings is the link between EI and stress management. A 2021 study published in *Frontiers in Psychology* demonstrated that individuals with higher EI are better equipped to handle stress, owing to their enhanced ability to regulate emotions and maintain a positive outlook during challenging situations. This ability to manage stress effectively is crucial for building equilibrium, as it allows individuals to recover more quickly from setbacks and maintain mental health. Additionally, advancements in neuroscience have provided deeper insights into the biological underpinnings of EI. Functional MRI studies have shown that emotionally intelligent individuals exhibit greater activation in brain regions associated with emotional regulation and empathy, such as the prefrontal cortex and the amygdala. This enhanced neural activity suggests that EI is not just a psychological construct but also a physiological one, deeply embedded in our brain's functioning. These findings, published in the *Journal of Neuroscience* in 2022, underscore the importance of nurturing EI for cognitive and emotional health. Recent research highlights the role of EI in professional success. A meta-analysis conducted by researchers at Harvard University in 2022 found that high EI is correlated with better leadership skills, improved job performance, and higher job satisfaction. This is attributed to emotionally intelligent individuals' ability to navigate complex social interactions, resolve conflicts effectively, and motivate team members. A study published in *Emotion* in 2023 demonstrated that participants who underwent an eight-week EI training program exhibited significant improvements in emotional regulation, empathy, and overall psychological adaptability. These findings suggest that EI can be developed and refined through targeted practices, making it a valuable focus for personal development initiatives. In this context, emotional intelligence is indispensable. It equips us with the tools to remain calm under pressure, bounce back from setbacks, and build stronger, more supportive relationships. High emotional intelligence allows us to better understand our emotional responses and those of others, fostering a more adaptive and resilient approach to life's difficulties.

Self-awareness is the foundation of emotional intelligence. It involves recognizing and understanding our own emotions, as well as how they influence our thoughts and behavior. Developing self-awareness requires regular self-reflection. One effective strategy for enhancing self-awareness is maintaining a journal. By regularly writing about our thoughts, feelings, and reactions, we can identify patterns and gain insights into our emotional triggers. For example, I found that journaling about my experiences during Michael's recovery helped me understand the sources of my stress and anxiety, enabling me to address them more effectively. **Self-regulation** is the ability to manage our emotions and impulses. It involves staying in control, even in stressful situations, and responding to challenges with a calm and measured approach. To develop self-regulation, I've found deep breathing to be incredibly effective. When faced with emotionally charged situations, such as during the difficult moments of Michael's rehabilitation, I practiced deep breathing to center myself and maintain composure. Additionally, reframing negative thoughts through cognitive restructuring helped me stay focused and positive. Intrinsic **motivation** is a key component of emotional intelligence. It involves having a passion for what you do, driven by internal rewards rather than external ones. Motivated individuals are more resilient because they are committed to their goals and can maintain a positive outlook despite setbacks. Setting personal goals and celebrating small achievements can enhance motivation. During the challenging times of my brother's recovery, setting incremental goals for his rehabilitation and celebrating each small victory kept us both motivated and optimistic. **Empathy** is the ability to understand and share the feelings of others. It involves recognizing emotional cues and responding appropriately, which strengthens interpersonal relationships and fosters a supportive environment. To develop empathy, active listening is crucial. When Michael expressed his frustrations and fears, I made a conscious effort to listen without judgment, acknowledging his feelings and providing emotional support. This not only strengthened our bond but also helped him feel understood and less isolated. **Social skills** involve the ability to communicate effectively, manage conflicts, and build strong relationships. These skills are essential for creating a support network.

Improving social skills requires practice in effective communication and conflict resolution. During difficult conversations, such as coordinating Michael's care with medical professionals, I focused on clear and empathetic communication, ensuring that everyone involved felt heard and understood. This approach helped us navigate complex situations more smoothly and collaboratively. One of the most profound examples of how emotional intelligence has benefited me occurred during a particularly challenging phase of Michael's recovery. He was undergoing a series of intensive physical therapy sessions that were both physically painful and emotionally draining. The frustration and despair he felt were palpable, and I, too, felt overwhelmed by the intensity of the situation. Drawing on my emotional intelligence, I first focused on self-awareness and self-regulation. I employed empathy. I sat down with Michael and encouraged him to share his feelings. I listened attentively, validating his emotions without offering immediate solutions or judgments. This act of empathetic listening helped him feel understood and supported. I also used my social skills to facilitate communication between Michael, myself, and his physical therapists. By fostering an open and collaborative dialogue, we were able to address Michael's concerns and adjust his therapy plan to better suit his needs. This not only improved his physical progress but also boosted his morale. Finally, motivation played a crucial role. We set small, achievable goals for each therapy session and celebrated every bit of progress, no matter how minor. This helped maintain a positive atmosphere and kept both of us focused on the ultimate goal of recovery. Through these strategies, I witnessed firsthand the power of emotional intelligence. Michael's journey was fraught with challenges, but by leveraging emotional intelligence, we navigated these obstacles with greater ease. As my experience with Michael's recovery has shown, emotional intelligence is a vital tool for overcoming adversity and fostering a resilient mindset.

Having a strong support network is crucial. Supportive relationships provide a safety net that helps us navigate life's challenges, offering emotional comfort, practical assistance, and a sense of belonging. When we face adversity, the presence of understanding and caring individuals can significantly buffer the negative effects of stress, helping us to recover more quickly and maintain our well-being. A robust support system not only aids in immediate crisis management but also fosters long-term strength by reinforcing our emotional health and stability. Seek out relationships that are positive, nurturing, and mutually supportive. Be intentional about spending time with people who lift you up and contribute to your emotional well-being. Join groups or communities where you can meet like-minded individuals who share your interests and values. Effective communication is the cornerstone of any strong relationship. Be open and honest with your friends and family about your needs, feelings, and boundaries. Encourage them to do the same, fostering an environment of trust and mutual respect. Listening attentively to others' concerns and experiences without judgment helps build deep, supportive connections. Show empathy and validate their feelings, which reinforces trust and strengthens your bond. Supportive relationships are built on reciprocity. Be there for others in their times of need, and don't hesitate to seek their support when you need it. This mutual give-and-take creates a balanced, resilient support network. Building and maintaining strong relationships requires time and effort. Regularly reach out to your friends and family, check in on their well-being, and make plans to spend quality time together. Consistent effort helps maintain strong, lasting connections. Not all relationships are beneficial. Be mindful of those that drain your energy or undermine your self-esteem. Setting boundaries with or distancing yourself from toxic individuals can protect your emotional health and make room for more supportive relationships. The journey following Michael's accident was fraught with uncertainty and emotional turmoil. It was during this time that I truly understood the power of a strong support network. When I first received the devastating news of Michael's accident, my initial reaction was one of overwhelming panic and helplessness. As I rushed to the hospital, I reached out to our close family members and friends. Their immediate and unwavering support provided a sense of stability amidst the chaos. My parents flew in from out of town, bringing with them not only physical help but also emotional strength that bolstered my resolve. One particularly challenging moment came when Michael faced a major setback in his rehabilitation. He was frustrated, and his spirits were low. It was during this difficult period that our friends rallied around us. A close friend, who happened to be a physical therapist, offered additional guidance and support, which proved invaluable. Another friend organized a small gathering at our home, providing a much-needed distraction and a reminder of the love and support surrounding us. These gestures, though seemingly small, had a profound impact. They reminded Michael and me that we were not alone in our struggle. The collective strength and encouragement from our support system gave us the emotional fortitude to push through the tough times. It was this network of caring individuals that helped transform moments of despair into opportunities for growth. Reflecting on these experiences, I am reminded of the African proverb, "If you want to go fast, go alone. If you want to go far, go together." The journey to recovery is undoubtedly a marathon, not a sprint. Surrounding ourselves with a strong support system ensures that we have the strength to endure and thrive, no matter what challenges come our way.

Emotional resilience is a skill that can be developed and strengthened through consistent practice. Here are some practical exercises and activities. Each exercise includes a step-by-step guide to implementation and examples of how my brother Michael and I have applied these practices in our own lives.

MINDFULNESS MEDITATION

Step-by-Step Guide:

1. **Find a Quiet Space:**
   - Choose a quiet, comfortable place where you won't be disturbed.

2. **Set a Timer:**
   - Start with just 5 minutes and gradually increase the time as you become more comfortable.

3. **Focus on Your Breath:**
   - Sit comfortably, close your eyes, and focus on your breath. Inhale deeply through your nose, hold for a few seconds, and exhale slowly through your mouth.

4. **Acknowledge and Release Thoughts:**
   - As thoughts arise, acknowledge them without judgment and gently bring your focus back to your breath.

Example: During the most stressful days of Michael's recovery, we set aside time each morning to practice mindfulness meditation together. This simple practice helped us start the day with a calm and centered mindset, making it easier to handle the challenges that arose.

GRATITUDE JOURNALING

Step-by-Step Guide:

1. **Choose a Journal:**
   - Select a notebook or digital platform for your gratitude journal.

2. **Set a Routine:**
   - Dedicate a few minutes each day, preferably in the morning or before bed, to write in your journal.

3. **List Three Things:**
   - Write down three things you are grateful for each day.

Example: During the challenging times of Michael's recovery, we both started keeping gratitude journals. Each evening, we would sit together and write down three things we were grateful for that day. This practice helped shift our focus from the difficulties we faced to the positive aspects of our lives, no matter how small. Over time, it became a cherished part of our routine, fostering a sense of appreciation and hope even on the toughest days.

PROGRESSIVE MUSCLE RELAXATION (PMR)

Step-by-Step Guide:

1. **Find a Comfortable Position:**

   ○ Sit or lie down in a comfortable position in a quiet space.

2. **Tense and Relax:**

   ○ Starting with your toes, tense each muscle group for five seconds and then relax them completely. Move gradually up your body, from your legs to your torso, arms, and finally your face.

3. **Breathe Deeply:**

   ○ Inhale deeply as you tense your muscles and exhale as you relax them.

Example: Progressive muscle relaxation became a nightly routine for Michael and me. This exercise helped reduce the physical tension and stress accumulated throughout the day, promoting better sleep and a sense of calm. It was especially useful after particularly strenuous physical therapy sessions.

COGNITIVE RESTRUCTURING

Step-by-Step Guide:

1. **Identify Negative Thoughts:**

    o   Write down any negative thoughts or beliefs you have during stressful situations.

2. **Challenge These Thoughts:**

    o   Examine the evidence for and against these thoughts. Are they based on facts or assumptions?

3. **Reframe with Positive Alternatives:**

    o   Replace the negative thoughts with more balanced and positive alternatives.

Example: After Michael's accident, I often found myself plagued with thoughts like, "We will never get through this." By challenging these thoughts and reframing them with positive alternatives such as, "We have the strength and resources to overcome this," I was able to maintain a more positive outlook and stay motivated during tough times.

BUILDING A SUPPORT SYSTEM

Step-by-Step Guide:

1. **Identify Your Network:**
   - List the people in your life who provide positive support, including friends, family, and colleagues.
2. **Reach Out Regularly:**
   - Make a conscious effort to connect with these individuals regularly. Schedule calls, meet for coffee, or simply check in via text.
3. **Offer and Ask for Support:**
   - Be willing to offer your support and don't hesitate to ask for help when you need it.

Example: During Michael's recovery, our support system was a crucial component. Regular check-ins with family and friends provided us with emotional support and practical assistance. One particular instance was when a friend organized a meal train, ensuring we had nutritious meals during the most hectic days. This act of kindness alleviated some of our stress and reminded us of the strength of our community.

PHYSICAL ACTIVITY

Step-by-Step Guide:

1. **Choose an Activity:**

    - Select a physical activity you enjoy, whether it's walking, running, yoga, or playing a sport.

2. **Set a Schedule:**

    - Incorporate this activity into your daily or weekly routine.

3. **Stay Consistent:**

    - Consistency is key. Aim to engage in physical activity at least three times a week.

Example: Michael and I integrated physical activity into our routine to boost. We started with gentle exercises, such as walking and stretching, and gradually progressed to more intensive activities as his strength improved. These sessions not only improved our physical health but also provided a much-needed mental break from the stress of recovery.

The methods shared in this chapter are designed to empower you to navigate life's challenges with greater ease and confidence. I encourage you to start small and be patient with yourself as you incorporate these practices. Remember, building it is a journey, not a destination. Each step you take towards understanding and managing your emotions is a step towards a more resilient and fulfilling life. As you embark on this journey, know that you are not alone. The experiences and practices shared here are not just theoretical; they are grounded in real-life applications that have helped me and my brother navigate some of our toughest times. By committing to these techniques, you are investing in your emotional health, equipping yourself to face whatever challenges come your way with strength and grace.

Part III: Enhancing Mental Performance

Enhanced Focus and Attention

Today, the ability to maintain focus has become an increasingly rare and valuable skill. The evolution of technology has brought unparalleled convenience and connectivity but has also introduced a multitude of distractions that can significantly impair our ability to concentrate. Historically, the concept of distraction has always been present. Ancient philosophers like Seneca and Marcus Aurelius wrote extensively about the importance of focus and mindfulness. However, the nature and scale of distractions have transformed dramatically with technological advancements. The invention of the printing press in the 15th century, for instance, revolutionized access to information, but even then, distractions were limited compared to today's standards. The 20th century saw the advent of radio and television, which began to shape the way people consumed information and entertainment. These media introduced new forms of distraction but still maintained a certain degree of passive engagement. The real paradigm shift came with the rise of the internet and, subsequently, the proliferation of digital devices in the 21st century. Smartphones, tablets, and laptops have become ubiquitous, embedding themselves in every aspect of our daily lives. With the introduction of the internet, the landscape of information consumption changed forever. The internet offers a vast, almost infinite repository of knowledge and entertainment at our fingertips. This unprecedented access to information, while beneficial, has also led to the phenomenon known as information overload. The sheer volume of available data can overwhelm our cognitive capacities, making it difficult to focus on a single task for extended periods. Social media platforms, which emerged in the early 2000s, have further exacerbated the issue of digital distractions. These platforms are designed to capture and retain user attention through endless feeds of content, notifications, and social interactions. The algorithm-driven nature of social media ensures that users are constantly bombarded with tailored content designed to maximize engagement, often at the expense of productivity and focus. Another significant development has been the rise of mobile technology. The smartphone, introduced in the mid-2000s, has become a central hub for communication, entertainment, and work. Its portability and multifunctionality mean that distractions are always just a tap away. Push notifications, instant messaging, and mobile applications contribute to an environment where interruptions are constant and pervasive. The workplace has not been immune to these changes. The integration of digital tools and platforms into professional settings has created new challenges for maintaining focus. Email, instant messaging, and collaboration tools, while enhancing productivity, also serve as continuous sources of distraction. The expectation of immediate responses and constant availability can fragment our attention and reduce our ability to engage deeply with tasks. Educational environments have also been transformed by digital technology. Students today face the challenge of balancing their studies with the myriad distractions presented by digital devices. The temptation to check social media, watch videos, or play games can detract from academic focus and performance. While these technological advancements have undoubtedly provided numerous benefits, they have also introduced significant challenges to our ability to maintain focus. Understanding the historical context of these distractions helps us appreciate the magnitude of the problem and sets the stage for exploring strategies to reclaim our attention in an increasingly connected world.

In the modern world, the ability to maintain focus is not just a desirable skill; it is a critical component of this journey. Recent research underscores the profound impact that focus has on our cognitive abilities, emotional well-being, and overall productivity.

A study conducted by the University of California, Irvine, found that it takes an average of 23 minutes and 15 seconds to regain focus after an interruption. This statistic highlights how distractions can significantly disrupt our workflow, leading to a substantial loss in productivity. The constant barrage of notifications and digital interruptions fragments our attention, making it difficult to engage deeply with tasks and think critically. The field of neuroscience provides further insights into why focus is so essential. Research by Dr. Daniel Goleman, a psychologist and author of "Focus: The Hidden Driver of Excellence," explains that the brain's prefrontal cortex, responsible for executive functions such as decision-making and problem-solving, is particularly susceptible to distractions. When our attention is divided, the prefrontal cortex struggles to maintain control, leading to decreased cognitive performance and impaired decision-making. A 2019 study published in the journal *Nature*

Communications revealed that multitasking can reduce productivity by up to 40%. The human brain is not designed to handle multiple tasks simultaneously. Instead, it switches rapidly between tasks, which increases cognitive load and decreases efficiency. This finding is crucial in understanding why sustained focus on a single task is far more effective than attempting to juggle multiple activities at once. Focus also plays a vital role in emotional resilience. Dr. Amishi Jha, a neuroscientist at the University of Miami, has conducted extensive research on mindfulness and attention. Her studies indicate that individuals who regularly practice it and focus exercises exhibit greater emotional stability. By training the mind to concentrate and remain present, individuals can better manage stress and recover more quickly from setbacks. In professional settings, the ability to maintain focus is directly linked to performance and success. A 2018 report from McKinsey & Company highlighted that high-performing employees often exhibit exceptional focus and deep work capabilities. These individuals can enter a state of flow, a term coined by psychologist Mihaly Csikszentmihalyi, where they become fully immersed in their tasks, leading to heightened creativity and productivity. It is integral to learning and skill acquisition. Research from the University of California, San Francisco, demonstrates that focused practice and deliberate attention are key factors in developing expertise. The brain's neuroplasticity allows it to form new connections and strengthen existing ones through repeated, focused practice. This principle is central to the concepts presented in "Peak Performance" by Brad Stulberg and Steve Magness, which emphasizes the importance of deep work and sustained focus in achieving high levels of performance. In the context of this field, focus helps individuals navigate the complexities and uncertainties of modern life. The ability to concentrate on what truly matters allows us to prioritize our efforts, make informed decisions, and maintain a sense of control amidst chaos. As we face an ever-increasing array of challenges, from economic instability to information overload, cultivating focus becomes a fundamental strategy. The latest research highlights how distractions undermine our cognitive abilities, emotional stability, and productivity. By understanding and addressing the impact of digital distractions, we can develop approaches to enhance our focus, ultimately leading to greater success and well-being. In an age where digital devices dominate our personal and professional lives, managing distractions has become a critical skill for maintaining focus and achieving peak performance. The omnipresence of smartphones, social media, and instant messaging creates a constant stream of interruptions that can severely impede our ability to concentrate. However, recent research offers several effective ones to combat these digital distractions. By implementing these techniques, you can reclaim your attention and improve your productivity. Here are some innovative and research-backed methods to help you stay focused amidst the digital noise.

A study by the American Psychological Association in 2020 found that **time blocking**—allocating specific blocks of time for different activities—significantly improves focus and productivity. By scheduling uninterrupted work periods and including "digital sabbaticals" where you disconnect from all devices, you can better manage distractions. For instance, designate certain hours in the day as "tech-free" to fully engage in deep work without digital interruptions. Utilize **technology to fight technology**. Tools like Freedom, StayFocusd, and Cold Turkey can block access to distracting apps and websites. A 2019 study in the *Journal of Behavioral Addictions* demonstrated that using such tools can reduce time spent on non-essential activities by up to 40%, allowing for more sustained focus on important tasks. Recent research from the University of Washington suggests that **turning off non-essential notifications** can drastically improve focus. Customizing notification settings to limit interruptions ensures that you only receive alerts for critical communications. This approach not only reduces distraction but also minimizes stress associated with constant digital pings. According to a 2021 study published in *Computers in Human Behavior*, **batch processing**—grouping similar tasks together and addressing them in dedicated time slots—can enhance cognitive performance. For example, set aside specific times of the day to check and respond to emails, rather than allowing them to interrupt you throughout the day. This method helps maintain a steady workflow and reduces the cognitive load associated with task switching. Inspired by Cal Newport's concept of digital minimalism, the **digital minimalism routine** technique involves intentionally simplifying your digital life. Recent studies, including one from the University of Cambridge in 2021, show that reducing the number of apps and digital platforms you engage with can significantly enhance focus. Evaluate which digital tools are essential and eliminate those that do not add value to your life or work.

Setting clear boundaries with technology is essential for maintaining focus and safeguarding our emotional well-being. As digital devices become more integrated into our daily routines, establishing limits can help us manage distractions and prioritize deep work. Creating **physical and temporal boundaries** can significantly reduce digital distractions. Research from the University of British Columbia in 2017 found that individuals who designated specific areas and times as tech-free experienced lower stress levels and higher productivity. For instance, make your bedroom a tech-free zone to improve sleep quality, or set aside the first hour of your workday for uninterrupted, device-free focus.A study published in *Sleep Health* in 2018 demonstrated that exposure to screens before bedtime negatively affects sleep quality and duration. Establishing a **digital curfew**—turning off all screens at least one hour before bed—can help improve sleep and ensure you wake up refreshed and ready to focus. Use this time to unwind with non-digital activities like reading a book or practicing mindfulness. Most smartphones and computers come with built-in **Do Not Disturb (DND)** modes that can mute notifications during specified times. Activating DND during work hours or important tasks can help you stay focused without the temptation of constant notifications. A 2019 study by the American Psychological Association found that using DND modes reduced distraction and improved task completion rates. Instead of letting digital interactions dictate your day, **schedule** specific times for checking emails, social media, and other digital activities. According to research from the *Journal of Applied Social Psychology* in 2020, individuals who scheduled tech breaks reported better concentration and task engagement. For example, allocate 15-minute breaks every two hours to catch up on digital communications, allowing you to focus on work without feeling disconnected. Informing colleagues, friends, and family about your tech **boundaries** can help reinforce them. Let others know when you will be unavailable due to focused work periods. A 2021 study in *Human Relations* highlighted that clear communication about availability can reduce the expectation of immediate responses and support a more focused work environment. Leverage technology to your advantage by using apps and tools designed to enhance focus and productivity. For instance, use calendar apps to block out dedicated work time, and employ focus-enhancing apps like Forest or Focus@Will to create a conducive work environment. These tools can help you manage your digital interactions more effectively. Starting your day without immediately diving into digital content can set a positive tone for the rest of the day. Research from the University of California, San Francisco, in 2021 found that individuals who began their mornings with non-digital activities, such as exercise or journaling, exhibited better focus and productivity throughout the day. A well-designed workspace can help you concentrate better and achieve your goals more efficiently. A 2020 study from the University of Exeter found that an organized and clutter-free workspace significantly enhances concentration and productivity. Arrange your desk to ensure that only essential items are within reach. Keep your workspace tidy and free from unnecessary clutter to reduce visual distractions. Ambient noise can be a major source of distraction. Research published in the *Journal of Environmental Psychology* in 2019 demonstrated that background noise negatively impacts cognitive performance. Consider using noise-canceling headphones or white noise machines to block out disruptive sounds. Alternatively, listen to focus-enhancing music or nature sounds, which have been shown to improve concentration and reduce stress. Proper lighting and ergonomic setup can significantly affect your ability to focus. A study by the American Society of Interior Designers in 2021 highlighted that natural light improves mood and productivity. Position your workspace near a window to take advantage of natural light, or use adjustable lamps to reduce eye strain. Ensure your chair and desk are ergonomically designed to promote comfort and prevent fatigue. Adding personal touches to your workspace can increase your sense of ownership and comfort, which in turn boosts focus. According to a 2018 study in the *Journal of Occupational Health Psychology*, personalized workspaces enhance job satisfaction and productivity. Incorporate items that inspire you, such as plants, artwork, or motivational quotes, but be mindful not to overdo it and create clutter. Embracing a minimalist approach to your workspace can help reduce distractions and improve focus. A 2019 study from the University of Toronto found that minimalist workspaces promote clarity of thought and better task management. Keep only the essentials on your desk and store other items out of sight to maintain a clean and distraction-free environment. If you work from home, it's essential to have a dedicated work area separate from your living spaces. A study by Stanford University in 2020 showed that having a designated workspace helps create a cognitive distinction between work and personal life, enhancing focus during work hours. Choose a quiet, comfortable area in your home where you can work without interruptions. Creating visual and physical boundaries within your workspace can help signal to others that you are in a focused work mode. This can include using partitions, closed doors, or even visual cues like signs indicating "do not disturb" periods. A 2019 study in *Applied Psychology* found that such boundaries reduce interruptions and improve concentration.

Over the years, I've honed several unique strategies to manage digital distractions and maintain focus. These techniques, refined through personal experience and informed by recent research, have been instrumental in enhancing my productivity. One of the most impactful ones I've implemented is the "Digital Sunset." Inspired by research from the *Journal of Sleep Research* in 2019, I turn off all screens and digital devices at least two hours before bedtime. This practice not only improves my sleep quality but also helps me wind down and mentally prepare for the next day. By establishing a clear boundary between my digital and personal life, I ensure that my evenings are peaceful and focused. To combat the constant interruptions of digital notifications, I created a system of "Focused Work Blocks." These are uninterrupted periods, typically 90 minutes long, dedicated to deep work. During these blocks, I use apps like Freedom to block distracting websites and silence my phone. Research by the *University of Illinois* in 2020 supports this approach, showing that working in extended, focused intervals enhances cognitive performance and creativity. Microbreaks help me reset and maintain a high level of concentration throughout the day. I start my day with a tech-free morning routine, dedicating the first hour after waking up to activities like exercise, journaling, or reading. This routine, backed by research from the *Journal of Occupational Health Psychology* in 2021, helps me set a positive tone for the day and primes my mind for focused work. By avoiding digital distractions first thing in the morning, I can preserve my inner clarity and energy for the tasks ahead. I've developed a system of environmental cues to signal when it's time to focus. For example, I light a specific scented candle when I begin a focused work session. This sensory cue, supported by research in *Cognitive Research: Principles and Implications* in 2020, helps condition my brain to enter a state of deep concentration. Additionally, I use a standing desk to alternate between sitting and standing, which keeps my energy levels up and prevents fatigue. At the end of each day, I spend 10 minutes reflecting on my productivity and identifying any distractions that hindered my focus. This reflection practice, informed by the principles of continuous improvement from *Peak Performance* by Stulberg and Magness, allows me to make necessary adjustments and refine them continually. We scattered information about mindfulness all throughout the book, but let's focus on it and delve in it in a little more "in-depth" kind of way: we are talking, at its core, of the practice of being fully present and engaged in the current moment. It involves observing your thoughts, emotions, and sensations without judgment, allowing you to respond to situations with clarity and intention rather than reacting impulsively. In recent years, it has gained widespread recognition for its profound benefits on mental health, cognitive function, and overall well-being. Its essence lies in its simplicity and accessibility. Unlike other practices that require specific tools or environments, it can be practiced anywhere, at any time. This flexibility makes it an ideal strategy for managing the complexities and demands of modern life. By focusing on the present moment, it helps to anchor our awareness, reducing the tendency to ruminate on the past or worry about the future. One of the most significant benefits is its impact on stress reduction. A landmark study published in the *Journal of Clinical Psychology* in 2018 found that regular awareness practice significantly reduces levels of cortisol, the body's primary stress hormone. By lowering cortisol levels, it helps to alleviate stress, promoting a sense of calm and relaxation. It also enhances emotional regulation. Research from the University of Toronto in 2019 demonstrated that mindfulness practitioners exhibit greater emotional stability. By observing their emotions without judgment, individuals can better understand and manage their emotional responses. This increased emotional intelligence leads to improved relationships, better decision-making, and a greater ability to cope with life's challenges. Its cognitive benefits are equally compelling. A study conducted by the University of California, Santa Barbara, in 2017 found that this kind of training enhances working memory and executive function. Participants who engaged in these exercises showed improved attention span, increased cognitive flexibility, and better problem-solving skills. These cognitive enhancements are particularly valuable in today's information-rich environment, where the ability to focus and process information efficiently is crucial. It also promotes physical health. A comprehensive review published in *Health Psychology Review* in 2020 highlighted that these exercises can lower blood pressure, improve sleep quality, and boost immune function. These physiological benefits are attributed to its stress-reducing effects, which in turn positively influence various bodily systems. In professional settings, it has been shown to enhance performance and productivity. A study by the *Journal of Occupational Health Psychology* in 2019 found that employees who practiced it reported higher job satisfaction, better interpersonal relationships, and increased work engagement. By fostering a mindful work environment, organizations can boost morale, reduce burnout, and improve overall performance. It also plays a critical role in fostering creativity and innovation. Research from the University of Groningen in 2018 demonstrated that it enhances divergent thinking, a key component of creative problem-solving. By promoting a state of open awareness, it allows individuals to approach challenges with a fresh perspective and generate novel solutions. It offers a wide array of benefits that extend across cognitive, emotional, and physical domains. Its ability to reduce stress, enhance cognitive function, and improve overall well-being makes it an invaluable tool in navigating the demands of modern life. Though often perceived as a modern phenomenon, it has deep historical roots that span across various cultures and traditions. Understanding its history provides a richer context for its contemporary practice and highlights its enduring relevance. Its origins can be traced back to ancient Eastern spiritual traditions, particularly Buddhism. Its concept, or "sati" in Pali, is a fundamental aspect of Buddhist teachings. It is one of the Seven Factors of Enlightenment and a core component of the Noble Eightfold Path, which outlines the practices leading to liberation from suffering. Mindfulness in Buddhism involves cultivating a heightened awareness of the present moment and an understanding of the nature of reality through meditation and ethical living. Buddhist awareness practices were first codified in the teachings of Siddhartha Gautama, known as the Buddha, around the 5th century BCE. The Satipatthana Sutta, a key Buddhist scripture, outlines four foundations: mindfulness of the body, feelings, mind, and irrational objects. These practices were designed to develop insight, ethical conduct, and intellectual discipline. While it is most commonly associated with Buddhism, similar practices can be found in other spiritual traditions. In Hinduism, the practice of "dhyana" or meditation focuses on achieving a state of concentrated awareness and inner peace. The Bhagavad Gita, a sacred Hindu text, emphasizes the importance of detached awareness and self-control, principles that align closely with the ones we just mentioned. In ancient China, Daoist practices also emphasized consciousness. Daoist meditation techniques aimed to harmonize the mind and body with the natural flow of the Dao, or the fundamental principle underlying the universe. Laozi, the legendary Daoist sage, advocated for simplicity, presence, and mindful living as paths to wisdom and balance. These practices have also been present in Western traditions, though under different names. The early Christian mystics, such as the Desert Fathers and Mothers of the 3rd century CE, practiced forms of contemplative prayer and meditation to cultivate inner stillness and divine presence. In Judaism, the practice of "hitbodedut," or self-seclusion, involves mindful prayer and reflection to connect with God. The modern awareness movement began in the 20th century, significantly influenced by the work of Jon Kabat-Zinn. In the late 1970s, Kabat-Zinn, a molecular biologist with a background in Buddhist meditation, developed the Mindfulness-Based Stress Reduction (MBSR) program at the University of Massachusetts Medical School. MBSR aimed to treat chronic pain and stress-related conditions through secular consciousness practices. Kabat-Zinn's work played a crucial role in bringing it into mainstream medicine and psychology. Since then, it has been extensively researched and integrated into various therapeutic modalities, including Mindfulness-Based Cognitive Therapy (MBCT) and Acceptance and Commitment Therapy (ACT). These approaches have been widely adopted in clinical settings to address mental health issues such as depression, anxiety, and post-traumatic stress disorder (PTSD). Today, it continues to evolve, with contemporary practices incorporating insights from neuroscience and psychology. The proliferation of awareness-based apps, online courses, and workplace programs reflects its growing popularity and accessibility. From its ancient roots in Eastern spiritual traditions to its modern applications in medicine and psychology, it has proven to be a timeless and universal practice. Its enduring presence and adaptation highlight its profound relevance and effectiveness in promoting well-being.

Drawing from my personal experiences and the latest research, I have developed a set of practices that are practical, effective, and easy to integrate into daily life. Here is a step-by-step guide to these practices:

Morning Mindfulness Ritual: Begin each day with a brief awareness session. Spend 5 minutes sitting quietly, focusing on your breath. Set an intention for the day, such as "I will approach today with patience and clarity." Perform a quick body scan to become aware of any tension or discomfort. Starting from the top of your head, slowly move your attention down to your toes, noticing any sensations without judgment. This helps to ground you and prepares your mind and body for the day ahead.

Mindful Breathing Exercise, 4-7-8 Breathing Technique: this technique, supported by research from the *Journal of Psychosomatic Research* in 2019, helps to calm the nervous system and reduce stress. Inhale deeply through your nose for a count of 4, hold the breath for a count of 7, and exhale slowly through your mouth for a count of 8. Repeat this cycle four times. This practice can be done anytime you feel stressed or overwhelmed.

Mindful Eating: During meals, take the time to fully engage with your food. Notice the colors, textures, and smells before taking a bite. Chew slowly and pay attention to the taste and sensation of the food in your mouth. This practice, backed by a 2018 study in *Appetite*, can improve digestion and promote healthier eating habits.

Mindful Walking: Incorporate cognizance into your daily walks. Pay attention to the sensation of your feet touching the ground, the movement of your body, and the sights and sounds around you. Walking meditation, as highlighted in a 2020 study in *Mindfulness*, can enhance inner clarity and reduce stress.

Mindfulness Microbreaks: Throughout the day, take short breaks to practice perception. Close your eyes, take a few deep breaths, and bring your awareness to the present moment. These microbreaks help to reset your focus and maintain productivity. Research from the University of Miami in 2018 supports the effectiveness of these brief sessions in reducing stress and enhancing concentration.

Evening Reflection: End your day with a practice that promotes positive emotions. Spend 5-10 minutes writing down three things you are grateful for that day. Reflect on why these things made you feel grateful and how they impacted your day. Studies published in the *Journal of Positive Psychology* in 2019 show that gratitude journaling can improve sleep quality and overall well-being.

Mindful Sleep Preparation: Create a calming pre-sleep routine that incorporates it. Dim the lights, disconnect from digital devices, and engage in a relaxing activity such as reading or gentle stretching. Spend a few minutes practicing mindful breathing or body scan meditation to prepare your mind and body for restful sleep.

Enhancing focus and attention is more critical now than ever before. With the relentless pace of modern life and the constant barrage of digital distractions, staying focused can feel like a superpower. Let me share a more personal and in-depth look into how it has significantly boosted focus and attention for me and others, providing concrete examples of its transformative impact.

Samantha, a project manager at a fast-paced marketing firm, found herself overwhelmed by constant emails, meetings, and tight deadlines. Her productivity was suffering, and she struggled to maintain focus during critical tasks. After attending a productivity workshop, Samantha decided to integrate specific strategies into her daily routine. She began by implementing time blocking, a technique where she allocated specific periods for different tasks throughout her day. By dedicating uninterrupted time slots for focused work, meetings, and breaks, Samantha was able to manage her schedule more effectively. She also used a physical planner to outline her daily goals and track her progress, which helped her stay organized and on task. In addition to time blocking, Samantha adopted the use of app and website blockers to minimize digital distractions. She installed software that restricted access to non-work-related websites during her designated work periods. This reduction in digital interruptions allowed her to maintain sustained focus on her projects. Samantha also improved her workspace by creating a distraction-free environment. She decluttered her desk, ensured proper lighting, and used noise-canceling headphones to block out office chatter. These changes enhanced her ability to concentrate and complete tasks more efficiently. Over time, Samantha noticed a significant increase in her productivity and decision-making abilities, leading to improved performance and recognition from her superiors.

David, a university student majoring in engineering, struggled with maintaining concentration during his long study sessions. The constant influx of notifications from his phone and social media made it challenging to stay focused on his coursework. Seeking a solution, David explored various approaches to enhance his academic performance. David started by creating a structured study schedule that incorporated regular breaks. He followed the principle of the Pomodoro Technique, working in focused intervals of 25 minutes followed by a five-minute break. This approach helped him manage his time effectively and prevented burnout during long study sessions. He also designated a specific study area in his apartment, free from distractions. By choosing a quiet corner with minimal visual stimuli, David created an environment conducive to concentration. He kept his study materials organized and within reach, reducing the time spent searching for books and notes. To further enhance his focus, David used digital tools such as app blockers to limit access to social media during study hours. He also employed productivity apps that tracked his study time and provided insights into his work habits. By analyzing this data, David was able to identify patterns and adjust his study techniques accordingly. David's dedication paid off. He noticed a marked improvement in his concentration and retention of information, leading to higher grades and a deeper understanding of his coursework. His professors and peers recognized his enhanced performance, which boosted his confidence and motivation.

Laura, a graphic designer at a busy advertising agency, often found it challenging to maintain focus under tight deadlines and constant creative demands. To overcome these challenges, Laura adopted several plans to enhance her focus and productivity. Laura began by establishing a daily routine that prioritized her most important tasks. She used the Eisenhower Matrix, a tool that helps categorize tasks based on their urgency and importance, to organize her workload. By tackling high-priority tasks first, Laura ensured that her most critical work received her best attention. To manage stress and maintain focus, Laura incorporated short physical activities into her day. She took brief walks, performed stretching exercises, and practiced desk yoga. These activities helped her recharge and maintain her concentration throughout the day. Laura also found that setting clear boundaries with her team improved her focus. She communicated her need for uninterrupted work periods and scheduled specific times for meetings and collaboration. This approach minimized unexpected interruptions and allowed her to dedicate focused time to her design projects. Laura was then able to enhance her creativity and meet tight deadlines with greater ease. Her ability to maintain focus under pressure led to higher quality work and increased client satisfaction.

The journey to mastering focus and attention through mindfulness is like learning to surf in a storm. The waves of distractions will keep coming, but with practice, you'll learn to ride them with grace and balance. Just like Samantha, David, and Laura, you can harness its power to transform your ability to concentrate and perform at your best. Imagine starting your day with a clear mind and a sense of purpose, like Samantha. Picture yourself breezing through study sessions with laser-sharp focus, like David. Envision handling tight deadlines and creative demands with ease, like Laura. These are not just stories but real-life examples of how it can revolutionize your life. The beauty of it lies in its simplicity. You don't need fancy equipment or hours of free time. Just a few minutes each day can make a world of difference. Whether it's a morning meditation, mindful breaks, or a structured routine, these small changes add up to significant improvements in your focus and overall well-being. And here's the best part: it isn't about achieving perfection. It's about progress. It's about becoming more aware of your thoughts and feelings and learning to navigate them without getting swept away. It's about finding calm amidst the chaos and turning challenges into opportunities for growth. So, take a deep breath. Start with one small step. Maybe it's setting an intention for the day or taking a mindful break between tasks. Whatever it is, commit to it and watch as your ability to focus and perform begins to flourish. Remember, the key to success is consistency and patience. As you embark on this journey, embrace the ups and downs. Celebrate your progress, no matter how small. And most importantly, be kind to yourself. After all, even the most seasoned surfers fall off their boards now and then. What matters is that you get back up and keep riding those waves. In the end, it is more than just a practice; it's a way of life. It's about living fully in each moment, making the most of every opportunity, and finding joy in the journey. So, go ahead, dive into the world of focus, and unlock your full potential. Your future self will thank you.

Optimizing Motivation

We're constantly bombarded with information at all times; notifications ping from our smartphones, emails flood our inboxes, and social media feeds demand our attention. This relentless stream of information, while beneficial in many ways, also poses a significant challenge: information overload. It can be difficult to stay focused and motivated when we're perpetually distracted and overwhelmed by the sheer volume of data coming our way. I recall a specific instance that vividly illustrates this challenge. A few years ago, I was juggling multiple projects, trying to keep up with the latest industry news, responding to endless emails, and staying active on social media to maintain my professional presence. Each day felt like a never-ending race against time. I would wake up early to get a head start, only to find myself buried under a mountain of information by mid-morning. My to-do list grew longer, and my motivation waned. I felt like I was constantly spinning my wheels but never making any real progress. One particularly overwhelming day, I had back-to-back meetings and a crucial project deadline. My phone buzzed incessantly with notifications, and my email inbox was overflowing. In the midst of trying to tackle my tasks, I received a news alert about an industry development. I felt compelled to read it immediately, fearing I might miss out on something important. As I skimmed the article, I realized I had lost track of time and was late for my next meeting. The constant influx of information had not only derailed my schedule but also sapped my motivation and energy. This experience forced me to confront the reality of information overload and its impact on my productivity and well-being. It was a wake-up call that led me to develop strategies to manage the deluge of information more effectively and reclaim my motivation. In the following sections, I'll share the insights and techniques that have helped me, and others I've coached, to navigate this digital age with renewed focus and drive.

The digital age's constant connectivity has fundamentally altered how we work and live. While it offers unprecedented access to information and instant communication, it also brings significant challenges. One of the most insidious is the impact on our motivation. The omnipresence of devices and platforms designed to capture our attention can severely disrupt our focus and productivity. Constant connectivity often leads to multitasking, which is hailed as a productivity booster but is, in reality, a motivation killer. Research has shown that multitasking reduces efficiency and performance because the brain can only focus on one task at a time. Each time we switch tasks, there is a cognitive cost. This phenomenon, known as "task-switching," can lead to mental fatigue, decreased productivity, and ultimately, a significant drop in motivation. Consider this: you start your day with a clear plan to work on an important project. However, as you settle in, your phone buzzes with notifications, your email pings with new messages, and your social media feeds beckon with updates. You might think you can handle it all simultaneously, but the reality is each distraction pulls you away from your primary task. This fragmented attention can make it feel like you're not making progress, leading to frustration and a decline in motivation. I've experienced this firsthand. During a critical phase of writing my first book, I found myself constantly interrupted by digital distractions. Every time I received a notification, I'd pause my writing to check it. This constant task-switching left me feeling scattered and unproductive. The frustration of not meeting my writing goals each day began to erode my motivation. I started dreading my writing sessions, which had once been a source of joy and fulfillment. Another example is from my coaching sessions. Many clients have shared how the barrage of information and the pressure to stay connected makes it hard to focus on long-term goals. They describe feeling overwhelmed by the need to constantly update their knowledge and skills, which leads to procrastination. This perpetual state of catch-up can drain their motivation, leaving them feeling stuck and disheartened.

The challenges of constant connectivity and multitasking are clear: they erode our ability to maintain sustained focus and diminish our motivation. Recognizing these challenges is the first step towards reclaiming our focus and driving sustained motivation. In the next section, I'll delve into practical plans for managing information overload and maintaining motivation amidst the digital deluge.

Navigating the sea of information in our digital age requires effective procedures to stay motivated and productive. Here are some proven methods for managing information overload, drawn from the latest research and my personal experiences. Effective time management is crucial in combating information overload. One effective approach is the **Eisenhower Matrix**, a decision-making tool that helps prioritize tasks based on their urgency and importance. Tasks are divided into four categories: urgent and important, important but not urgent, urgent but not important, and neither urgent nor important. By focusing on important tasks first, you ensure that your energy is directed toward meaningful work, enhancing your motivation and productivity. A digital detox is essential for resetting your brain and reducing the stress of constant connectivity. Start by identifying the digital habits that contribute to information overload. Are you constantly checking your phone? Do you have multiple tabs open while working? Awareness is the first step toward change. Implementing regular digital detox periods can significantly improve your inner clarity and motivation. For example, designate one day a week as a "digital detox day" where you disconnect from all non-essential digital devices. Use this time to engage in offline activities that rejuvenate you, such as reading a book, spending time outdoors, or pursuing a hobby. Another effective strategy is to limit your screen time before bed. Studies show that blue light from screens can interfere with your sleep cycle, leading to poor sleep quality and decreased motivation the next day. Create a bedtime routine that excludes screens at least an hour before you sleep. Instead, engage in relaxing activities like reading a physical book or practicing mindfulness. **Monotasking** can be another useful strategy. Unlike multitasking, which can scatter your focus, monotasking involves dedicating your attention to one task at a time. Research indicates that focusing on a single task enhances productivity and reduces mental fatigue. By immersing yourself fully in each task, you can complete work more efficiently and maintain higher levels of motivation. Setting clear boundaries for information consumption is vital in preventing overload. Begin by curating your information sources. Unsubscribe from newsletters, blogs, and social media feeds that don't add significant value. Instead, choose a few high-quality sources that align with your interests and professional needs. Establish specific times for checking emails and social media. Instead of responding to emails as they arrive, set aside designated times during the day for email correspondence. This prevents constant interruptions and allows you to focus on more meaningful tasks. For social media, consider using tools like "Do Not Disturb" or app timers to limit your usage. Another effective boundary-setting strategy is to create an **"information diet."** Just as you monitor your food intake for a healthy body, be selective about the information you consume for a healthy mind. Allocate time for deep, focused reading on subjects that matter to you, and avoid the temptation of endless scrolling and clickbait content. Finally, consider adopting a "mindful consumption" approach. Before consuming any piece of information, ask yourself: Is this relevant to my goals? Will it add value to my work or personal life? By being intentional about your information intake, you can significantly reduce the noise and maintain your motivation. Implementing these can help you manage the overwhelming influx of information in today's digital world. By mastering time management, engaging in regular digital detoxes, and setting firm boundaries for information consumption, you can reclaim your focus, enhance your productivity, and sustain your motivation amidst the digital deluge. Prioritizing tasks is not just a productivity hack; it's a necessity for maintaining motivation and achieving meaningful progress. When faced with a seemingly endless list of tasks and constant distractions, it's easy to feel overwhelmed and unmotivated. However, with effective prioritization, you can regain control and ensure that your efforts are directed toward what truly matters. One of the foundational principles of effective prioritization is understanding the **Pareto Principle**, or the 80/20 rule. This principle suggests that 80% of your results come from 20% of your efforts. Identifying and focusing on those key tasks that drive the majority of your outcomes can drastically improve your productivity and motivation. For instance, if you're managing a project, pinpoint the critical activities that will propel the project forward and prioritize those over less impactful tasks. This not only maximizes your efficiency but also provides a clear sense of direction and accomplishment. Another practical method is **task batching**, which involves grouping similar tasks together and tackling them in dedicated time blocks. This approach minimizes the mental fatigue associated with constant task-switching and helps maintain a steady workflow. For example, allocate specific times for checking emails, making phone calls, and conducting meetings, rather than interspersing these activities throughout the day. This concentrated focus on related tasks can enhance your efficiency and keep you motivated by creating a rhythm in your workday. **Setting SMART goals** (Specific, Measurable, Achievable, Relevant, Time-bound) is another critical aspect of prioritization which was previously mentioned in another chapter. Clear, attainable goals provide a roadmap for your tasks, breaking down larger objectives into manageable steps. For instance, if your goal is to write a comprehensive report, set specific milestones for research, drafting, and editing. By achieving these smaller goals, you maintain a sense of progress and momentum, which is vital for sustained motivation. The **ABCDE Method** is also highly effective for prioritization. This technique involves categorizing tasks into five levels of importance:

A tasks: Must be done (highest priority)

B tasks: Should be done (next in line)

C tasks: Nice to do (not urgent or important)

D tasks: Delegate if possible

E tasks: Eliminate if unnecessary

By systematically addressing A tasks first, you ensure that your most critical objectives are met, which boosts your motivation as you see tangible results. This method helps you avoid the trap of spending too much time on low-priority tasks that do not significantly contribute to your goals. Leveraging technology can further enhance your prioritization efforts. Apps like **Todoist** and **Trello** enable you to organize tasks, set deadlines, and visualize your progress. These tools can serve as external aids to keep you on track, reminding you of your priorities and helping you stay focused on your key tasks. Incorporating these prioritization techniques into your daily routine can transform how you manage your workload. By focusing on the most impactful tasks, organizing your activities effectively, and leveraging technology, you can overcome the challenges of information overload, maintain high levels of motivation, and achieve your goals with greater efficiency and satisfaction.

The environment in which you work plays a crucial role in maintaining motivation. Creating a conducive environment can enhance focus, reduce stress, and boost overall productivity. Start by **decluttering your workspace**. A clean and organized workspace can significantly reduce distractions and help you focus on your tasks. Remove any unnecessary items from your desk and keep only essential tools and documents. This minimalist approach not only makes your workspace visually appealing but also mentally refreshing. **Personalizing your workspace** can also boost motivation. Surround yourself with items that inspire and motivate you, such as photos, quotes, or plants. These personal touches can create a positive atmosphere and remind you of your goals and aspirations. **Optimizing lighting** is another key factor. Natural light has been shown to improve mood and energy levels, enhancing productivity. If natural light is limited, consider using a desk lamp with adjustable brightness to reduce eye strain and create a comfortable working environment. Studies suggest that exposure to natural light can increase alertness and reduce the feeling of fatigue, thereby maintaining high motivation levels throughout the day. **Ergonomics** plays a significant role in maintaining physical comfort and preventing fatigue. Ensure that your chair and desk are at the correct height to support good posture. An ergonomic chair, keyboard, and mouse can prevent physical discomfort, allowing you to focus better on your tasks. Taking regular breaks to stretch and move around can also prevent burnout and maintain motivation. Incorporating **nature elements** into your workspace can enhance well-being and motivation. Studies have shown that plants in the workspace can reduce stress and increase productivity. If space allows, add a few plants to your desk or office.

Even a small potted plant can make a difference. Finally, establish a **routine** that signals the start and end of your workday. Having a set routine can create a sense of structure and help you transition into a focused work mode. This could include a morning ritual, such as a short meditation session, and an end-of-day routine, like reviewing your accomplishments and planning for the next day. These routines can provide a cognitive reset and keep you motivated to tackle new challenges each day. Implementing these approaches can help you stay on track, maintain high energy levels, and achieve your goals with greater efficiency and satisfaction. Throughout my career, I've relied on prioritization to stay motivated and productive amidst overwhelming demands. One particular instance was during the writing of my first book. Faced with tight deadlines and a flood of information, I used the Pareto Principle to identify key chapters that required immediate attention. By focusing on these critical sections, I made significant progress and avoided the paralyzing effects of information overload. In my coaching practice, I've seen similar success. One client, struggling with constant distractions, adopted task batching and the ABCDE Method. By grouping similar tasks and prioritizing A tasks, she transformed her work habits. Her productivity soared, and she felt more in control and motivated. These strategies not only improved our productivity but also reignited our motivation by providing a clear path to achieving our goals. Implementing these techniques can help anyone navigate the complexities of the digital age with greater focus and determination.

Understanding motivation is crucial for personal and professional development. Motivation can be broadly categorized into two types: intrinsic and extrinsic motivation. **Intrinsic motivation** refers to engaging in an activity for its inherent satisfaction rather than for some separable consequence. When you are intrinsically motivated, you perform an activity because it is enjoyable or interesting, not because of external pressures or rewards. For example, someone might play the piano simply because they love the music and the process of creating it. This type of motivation is driven by internal rewards, such as a sense of accomplishment or the joy of the activity itself. On the other hand, **extrinsic motivation** involves performing an activity to achieve an external goal or reward. This could include things like working for a paycheck, studying to get good grades, or exercising to lose weight. Extrinsic motivation is fueled by the desire for external rewards or to avoid negative consequences. While this type of motivation can be powerful, it is often dependent on external factors that may not always be within your control. Understanding the difference between intrinsic and extrinsic motivation is essential because it influences how we approach tasks and maintain motivation over time. Intrinsic motivation tends to be more sustainable and leads to higher levels of satisfaction and engagement. When you are intrinsically motivated, you are more likely to persist in the face of challenges and experience greater fulfillment from your efforts. However, extrinsic motivation can be highly effective for achieving specific goals, especially in the short term. By recognizing when to leverage intrinsic versus extrinsic motivators, you can tailor your approach to different tasks and situations, maximizing your overall motivation and effectiveness. Balancing both types of motivation can help you stay driven and achieve a well-rounded sense of accomplishment and satisfaction in your endeavors. Intrinsic motivation stems from within. It is the drive to engage in an activity because it is inherently enjoyable, satisfying, or interesting. Unlike extrinsic motivation, which is fueled by external rewards or pressures, intrinsic motivation is about the pleasure and fulfillment derived from the activity itself. One of the key characteristics of intrinsic motivation is **autonomy**. When you are intrinsically motivated, you feel a sense of control over your actions. You choose to engage in an activity because you want to, not because you have to. For instance, a person who loves painting may spend hours creating art simply because they find joy in the process, not because they are seeking praise or financial gain. Another characteristic is **competence**. Intrinsically motivated individuals often seek to improve their skills and master challenges. This sense of growth and achievement fuels their motivation. For example, a student might study a subject extensively because they are fascinated by it and enjoy the challenge of learning more, rather than just aiming for high grades. **Relatedness** also plays a role in intrinsic motivation. Engaging in activities that foster a sense of connection with others can be intrinsically motivating. For example, participating in a community garden project might be driven by a love for gardening and the joy of working alongside others who share the same passion. Examples of intrinsic motivation are abundant. Consider a writer who spends countless hours crafting stories because they love the creative process. An athlete who trains tirelessly because they enjoy the sport itself, not just winning medals, exemplifies intrinsic motivation. Similarly, a software developer might work on open-source projects out of pure interest and the desire to contribute to the community, not for monetary compensation. The benefits of intrinsic motivation are profound and far-reaching, impacting both personal satisfaction and professional success. In personal life, intrinsic motivation leads to **greater satisfaction and well-being**. When you engage in activities you genuinely enjoy, you experience higher levels of happiness and fulfillment. This positive emotional state contributes to overall mental health and reduces stress. For instance, hobbies pursued out of genuine interest, such as playing a musical instrument, hiking, or cooking, can provide a sense of relaxation and joy, enriching your personal life. Intrinsic motivation also fosters **creativity and innovation**. When you are driven by internal satisfaction, you are more likely to think outside the box and explore new ideas. This creative freedom can lead to unique and innovative solutions to problems. For example, many groundbreaking inventions and artistic masterpieces were created by individuals driven by a deep-seated passion for their work. In the professional realm, intrinsic motivation translates to **higher engagement and productivity**. Employees who find their work inherently rewarding are more likely to be engaged and committed. They tend to put in more effort, show greater perseverance, and produce higher-quality work. For instance, a teacher who loves educating children will go above and beyond to make lessons engaging and impactful, resulting in better student outcomes. **Intrinsic motivation also promotes lifelong learning and**

skill development. When you are genuinely interested in a subject, you are more likely to invest time and effort into learning and improving. This continuous pursuit of knowledge and growth is crucial in today's rapidly changing world. For example, a software engineer who loves coding will keep up with the latest technologies and continuously enhance their skills, making them more valuable in the job market. It can lead to **better relationships and teamwork**. When you are passionate about your work, it can inspire and motivate those around you. This positive energy can foster a collaborative and supportive work environment. For instance, a manager who is genuinely enthusiastic about their projects can create a motivated team that works well together to achieve common goals. Finally, intrinsic motivation is linked to **resilience and perseverance**. When you are intrinsically motivated, you are more likely to persist through challenges and setbacks because you derive satisfaction from the activity itself, not just the outcome. This is crucial for achieving long-term goals. For example, an entrepreneur passionate about their business idea will continue to push forward despite obstacles, driven by their love for what they do. By understanding and nurturing this type of motivation, you can achieve greater satisfaction, foster creativity, improve productivity. Engaging in activities that you find inherently rewarding not only enriches your life but also inspires those around you, creating a positive and motivating environment.

Extrinsic motivation arises from external factors rather than internal satisfaction. It is driven by the desire to achieve external rewards or avoid negative consequences. This type of motivation can be powerful and effective, especially in structured environments where specific outcomes are desired. One of the key characteristics of extrinsic motivation is **external rewards**. These rewards can take many forms, such as money, grades, praise, awards, or social recognition. For example, a student might study diligently to achieve high grades and gain praise from parents and teachers, rather than for the love of learning itself. Similarly, an employee might work overtime to earn a bonus or a promotion, driven by the financial reward and recognition rather than intrinsic interest in the task. **Compliance and adherence** are also significant aspects of extrinsic motivation. People often engage in activities to meet external expectations or avoid penalties. For instance, a person might adhere to workplace policies and procedures to avoid disciplinary actions, or a child might complete chores to avoid punishment from parents. **Competition** is another characteristic associated with extrinsic motivation. The desire to outperform others and gain recognition can be a strong motivator. Athletes often compete fiercely, driven by the prospect of winning medals, trophies, or public acclaim. This competitive drive is fueled by the external validation and rewards that come with being the best. Examples of extrinsic motivation are prevalent in various aspects of life. In the workplace, sales professionals might be motivated by commissions and performance bonuses. In education, students often strive for scholarships and academic awards. In sports, athletes aim for medals, trophies, and endorsements. Even in personal life, individuals might engage in fitness routines to receive compliments on their appearance or achieve a certain body image. Extrinsic rewards can be potent drivers of behavior, influencing people to perform tasks and reach goals that they might not pursue based solely on intrinsic motivation. Understanding how extrinsic rewards work can help in designing effective motivational approaches in various settings. One-way extrinsic rewards drive behavior is through **reinforcement**. Positive reinforcement involves providing a reward following a desired behavior, increasing the likelihood that the behavior will be repeated. For example, a company might offer performance bonuses to employees who exceed their targets, reinforcing high productivity and encouraging continued effort. Negative reinforcement, on the other hand, involves removing an unpleasant consequence when the desired behavior occurs. For instance, a manager might relieve an employee from less favorable tasks as a reward for achieving a difficult goal, thus reinforcing the achievement. **Incentive systems** are widely used in organizational settings to motivate employees. These systems are based on the principle that behavior can be directed and influenced by structured rewards. For example, a sales team might be offered tiered commissions, where higher sales volumes lead to progressively larger bonuses. This creates a clear and direct link between effort, performance, and reward, motivating employees to strive for higher performance levels. Extrinsic rewards can also foster **goal-oriented behavior**. When individuals have clear, tangible rewards to work towards, they are often more focused and driven. The prospect of these rewards provides a clear goal and encourages sustained effort and perseverance. However, it is essential to recognize the potential downsides of relying solely on extrinsic motivation. Overemphasis on external rewards can sometimes lead to a phenomenon known as the **overjustification effect**, where intrinsic motivation diminishes because the task is seen only as a means to an end. For example, if a student who loves reading is constantly rewarded with money for each book read, they might start valuing reading only for the financial reward, rather than for the pleasure of reading itself. To mitigate this, it's crucial to balance extrinsic and intrinsic motivators. For example, while offering bonuses for performance, employers can also foster a positive work environment where employees feel valued and find intrinsic satisfaction in their work. Encouraging personal growth, recognizing achievements, and providing opportunities for meaningful work can enhance intrinsic motivation alongside extrinsic rewards. Extrinsic rewards can also be used strategically to **initiate behavior** that might eventually lead to intrinsic motivation. For instance, rewarding children for practicing a musical instrument can encourage them to develop a habit and skill. Over time, as they become more proficient, they might start to enjoy playing and find intrinsic satisfaction in it, reducing the need for external rewards. While powerful and effective, it should be balanced with intrinsic motivation to sustain long-term engagement and satisfaction. By understanding and strategically leveraging extrinsic motivators, individuals and organizations can enhance performance and achieve desired outcomes while fostering an environment where intrinsic motivation can flourish.

To achieve sustained motivation and high performance, it's essential to balance and leverage both intrinsic and extrinsic motivation.

Combining these two types of motivation can lead to a more fulfilling and effective approach to personal and professional tasks. Ensure that external rewards are meaningful and aligned with personal values and interests. For instance, if you're motivated by learning, seek out job roles or projects that offer opportunities for skill development and growth, while also providing financial incentives. This alignment helps maintain intrinsic interest while benefiting from extrinsic rewards. Foster a work or learning environment that supports both types of motivation. Recognize and reward achievements (extrinsic) while also encouraging autonomy, mastery, and purpose (intrinsic). For example, a manager could offer performance bonuses (extrinsic) and simultaneously provide employees with challenging projects that allow them to develop new skills and take ownership of their work (intrinsic). Establish goals that provide both intrinsic satisfaction and extrinsic rewards. For instance, aim to complete a project because it's intellectually stimulating and aligns with your passions (intrinsic) and also because it leads to a promotion or bonus (extrinsic). This dual-outcome approach keeps you engaged and motivated on multiple levels. Initially, extrinsic rewards can be used to encourage participation in an activity, with the aim of developing intrinsic motivation over time. For example, offering children rewards for reading can help them develop a habit and eventually find joy and interest in reading itself.

Let's look over some examples: a software developer is offered a bonus for completing a project ahead of schedule (extrinsic). Simultaneously, the project involves using new technologies that the developer is passionate about and eager to learn (intrinsic). This combination keeps the developer motivated by both the financial reward and the opportunity for personal growth. A student is motivated to excel in exams due to the promise of a scholarship (extrinsic). At the same time, the subjects they are studying are ones they find fascinating and enjoy learning about (intrinsic). This balance helps the student stay committed and enthusiastic about their studies. An individual might start a fitness regimen with the goal of losing weight to look better for an upcoming event (extrinsic). As they progress, they begin to enjoy the physical activity itself, experiencing increased energy and well-being (intrinsic). The initial external goal helps kickstart the process, while the intrinsic enjoyment ensures long-term commitment. A volunteer joins a community project to gain recognition and enhance their resume (extrinsic). Over time, they find deep satisfaction in helping others and making a positive impact (intrinsic). This intrinsic fulfillment encourages continued involvement, even when the initial external rewards are no longer the primary motivator. By thoughtfully combining intrinsic and extrinsic motivators, you can create a more robust and sustainable motivation framework. This balanced approach not only drives immediate performance but also fosters long-term engagement and satisfaction, leading to personal and professional growth.

Throughout my career, I've harnessed both intrinsic and extrinsic motivation to achieve success and fulfillment. For example, I pursued challenging projects that not only offered financial rewards but also aligned with my passion for innovation. This balance kept me motivated through both monetary incentives and personal growth. For readers, my advice is to align your tasks with your interests and values while setting tangible rewards for milestones. Seek out roles or projects that offer both intrinsic satisfaction and extrinsic benefits. This approach will help you stay motivated, achieve your goals, and find greater satisfaction in your endeavors.

Decision Efficiency

In our modern world, decision efficiency has become more critical than ever. We live in an era where information overload, rapid technological advancements, and constant changes define our daily lives. The ability to make quick and effective decisions can mean the difference between success and failure, particularly in high-stress environments. This chapter will delve into the art and science of making rapid decisions in uncertain times, a skill that I have honed through personal experience and professional practice. My journey into understanding the importance of decision efficiency began unexpectedly. I vividly remember the day I received the call about my brother Michael's accident. In an instant, my world turned upside down. As I rushed to the hospital, a whirlwind of emotions and thoughts clouded my mind. Fear, uncertainty, and a sense of helplessness threatened to overwhelm me. Yet, amidst the chaos, I realized that I needed to make swift and clear-headed decisions to support my brother and navigate the challenges ahead. This experience was a turning point. It taught me that in moments of crisis, the ability to quickly assess a situation, weigh options, and make decisions is invaluable. It wasn't just about making choices under pressure; it was about making the right choices that could lead to the best possible outcomes. My brother's journey to recovery was a testament to the power of decisive action, and it inspired me to delve deeper into the mechanics of decision-making. In my professional life as a coach and mentor, I have encountered numerous individuals struggling with decision paralysis. Whether it's an executive facing a critical business decision or an athlete determining the best course of action in a game, the underlying challenge remains the same: how to make rapid and effective decisions when the stakes are high. Over the years, I have developed and refined policies to help others overcome this challenge, drawing from both personal experiences and a wealth of research. Decision efficiency is not just about speed; it's about accuracy and confidence. It's about having the tools and mindset to navigate uncertainty with clarity and purpose. In the following sections, we will explore various techniques to enhance your decision-making capabilities. From understanding the psychology of decision-making to practical tools for rapid assessment, this chapter aims to equip you with the skills needed to thrive in an unpredictable world. As we embark on this exploration, I will share insights from my own journey and those of others who have faced similar challenges. Through these stories, I hope to illustrate that decision efficiency is not an innate talent but a skill that can be developed and mastered. By the end of this chapter, you will have a deeper understanding of how to make quick, effective decisions that lead to success, even in the most uncertain of times.

In an era characterized by rapid change and uncertainty, making decisions has become increasingly complex. The traditional decision-making frameworks, which relied on stable environments and predictable outcomes, are often inadequate in today's dynamic world. As I reflect on my own experiences and those of the individuals I've coached, it becomes evident that the ability to navigate uncertainty is not just a valuable skill—it's a necessity. One of the primary challenges of making decisions in a constantly changing environment is the sheer volume of information available. We are bombarded with data from all directions, much of which is conflicting or ambiguous. This information overload can lead to analysis paralysis, where the fear of making the wrong decision prevents us from making any decision at all. In my coaching practice, I often encounter clients who are stuck in this paralysis, unable to move forward because they are overwhelmed by the possibilities and consequences. A key example from my own life illustrates this challenge vividly. After my brother's accident, we were faced with numerous medical decisions, each with significant implications for his recovery. The doctors presented us with various treatment options, each backed by different statistics and potential outcomes. The pressure to make the right choice was immense, and the stakes could not have been higher. At that moment, I realized that waiting for perfect clarity was not an option. We had to make the best decision we could with the information available and be prepared to adapt as new information emerged. This experience underscored a critical lesson: in uncertain times, decision-making is an iterative process. It involves making informed choices quickly, monitoring the outcomes, and being ready to adjust as the situation evolves. This approach, often referred to as "dynamic decision-making," is essential in fast-paced environments where waiting for all the facts can result in missed opportunities or exacerbated problems. In my coaching career, I've seen how embracing this dynamic approach can transform decision-making under pressure. One of my clients, a CEO of a tech startup, was navigating the volatile landscape of the industry. He struggled with making decisions because the market conditions were constantly shifting. Together, we worked on developing a framework that allowed him to make rapid decisions with the understanding that these decisions were not set in stone. Instead, they were checkpoints in an ongoing process of assessment and adaptation. This mindset shift enabled him to lead his company more effectively, responding to changes swiftly and with greater confidence. Another challenge in uncertain times is the emotional component of decision-making. Fear, anxiety, and stress can cloud our judgment and lead to decisions based on short-term relief rather than long-term benefit. When Michael was in the ICU, the emotional toll was overwhelming. There were moments when the fear of losing him made it difficult to think rationally. However, it was during these times that I learned the importance of grounding myself. Another crucial aspect of decision-making in uncertain times is the ability to distinguish between what is within our control and what is not. This concept, rooted in Stoic philosophy, has been a guiding principle in my life and work. When faced with uncertainty, it's easy to get caught up in factors beyond our control, leading to frustration and helplessness. Instead, focusing on what we can control—our actions, responses, and mindset—empowers us to make more effective decisions. A powerful example of this comes from a client who was a senior executive at a multinational corporation. She was dealing with a crisis that had global implications and felt overwhelmed by the uncontrollable external factors. We worked on identifying the elements of the situation that she could influence to address those proactively. This shift in focus not only improved her decision-making but also enhanced her leadership during a turbulent time.

Making decisions in uncertain times requires a combination of information management, emotional balance and a focus on controllable factors. By embracing a dynamic approach to decision-making, grounding ourselves emotionally, and concentrating on what we can influence, we can navigate uncertainty with greater confidence and effectiveness. Through my own experiences and those of my clients, I've seen firsthand how these strategies can transform decision-making from a daunting task into a powerful tool for success. Effective decision-making under pressure requires a blend of practical plans and a mindset that embraces adaptability. In this section, I'll outline several ones for quick decision-making.

The OODA Loop, developed by military strategist John Boyd, stands for Observe, Orient, Decide, and Act. This iterative decision-making process is designed for rapid adaptation in changing environments. Here's how it works:

Observe: Collect current information from the environment.

Orient: Analyze the information and update your psychological models.

Decide: Determine a course of action based on your analysis.

Act: Implement the decision and observe the results.

During my brother Michael's recovery, we often had to make quick decisions about his treatment. By applying the OODA Loop, we could swiftly gather information from medical staff, orient ourselves to the new data, decide on the next steps, and act. This approach minimized delays and allowed us to continuously adjust our strategy as new information became available.

Heuristics are mental shortcuts that allow for quick decision-making. While they are not foolproof, they are invaluable when time is of the essence. One effective heuristic is the "satisficing" approach—opting for a solution that is good enough rather than perfect. In my coaching career, I worked with a marketing executive who struggled with decision paralysis when launching new campaigns. By adopting the satisficing heuristic, she focused on identifying solutions that met the essential criteria without being bogged down by perfectionism. This shift allowed her to launch campaigns more efficiently and adapt based on real-time feedback.

Rapid prototyping, commonly used in product development, can be a valuable decision-making tool. This approach involves quickly creating a preliminary version of a solution to test and refine it based on feedback. It emphasizes action and iteration over prolonged deliberation. A client in the tech industry faced a critical decision about launching a new software feature. Instead of spending months in planning and development, we adopted a rapid prototyping approach. By quickly developing a basic version of the feature, they could test it with a select group of users, gather feedback, and make informed decisions about further development. This not only sped up the decision-making process but also reduced the risk of failure by incorporating real-world insights early on.

The DECIDE model, often used in healthcare, is a systematic approach to decision-making:

Define the problem.

Establish criteria.

Consider alternatives.

Identify the best option.

Develop and implement a plan.

Evaluate the outcome.

A case from my coaching experience involved a startup founder facing a critical pivot decision. By guiding him through the DECIDE model, we clearly defined the challenges, established criteria for success, considered various pivot options, identified the best path forward, implemented the pivot, and continuously evaluated the results. This structured approach helped the founder navigate a pivotal moment with confidence.

Decision trees are visual representations of possible choices and their outcomes. They are particularly useful for breaking down complex decisions into manageable parts. By mapping out options and potential consequences, decision trees help clarify the path forward. In a consulting project with a nonprofit organization, we used decision trees to navigate funding decisions. The organization faced multiple funding opportunities, each with different implications. By visually mapping out each option and its potential outcomes, the team could make informed, rapid decisions about which funding avenues to pursue.

Pre-mortem analysis, introduced by psychologist Gary Klein, involves imagining that a decision has failed and working backward to determine what could lead to that failure. This proactive approach helps identify potential pitfalls and allows for contingency planning. When I was preparing to launch a new coaching program, we conducted a pre-mortem analysis. By envisioning possible reasons for failure—such as inadequate marketing or insufficient participant engagement—we developed strategies to mitigate these risks. This preparation enabled us to launch the program smoothly and adjust swiftly as needed.

Creating a **culture that encourages rapid decision-making** is crucial. This involves empowering team members to make decisions, providing them with the necessary tools and information, and fostering an environment where quick, informed decisions are valued. One of my corporate clients, a mid-sized tech firm, struggled with slow decision-making due to a hierarchical structure. By fostering a culture of empowerment and providing decision-making frameworks, the company significantly improved its responsiveness and adaptability. Team members felt more confident in making rapid decisions, leading to increased innovation and productivity.

By embracing approaches like the OODA Loop, heuristics, the Eisenhower Matrix, the DECIDE model, the Two-Minute Rule, decision trees, pre-mortem analysis, and fostering a decision-making culture, we can navigate uncertainty with greater confidence and effectiveness. These plans, informed by both personal experiences and professional practice, provide a robust toolkit for anyone seeking to improve their decision-making efficiency. Through continuous learning and application, we can transform decision-making from a daunting task into a powerful asset for success.

High-pressure situations demand not only rapid decision-making but also effective problem-solving skills. Enhancing these skills requires a combination of cerebral policies, practical techniques, and a resilient mindset. In this section, I will discuss various systems to improve problem-solving under pressure, enriched with personal experiences and insights from working with others. Maintaining composure is critical when facing high-pressure situations. Panic and anxiety can cloud judgment and impair problem-solving abilities. One technique to stay calm is **controlled breathing**. Deep, rhythmic breathing helps lower stress levels and enhances focus. During my brother's rehabilitation, there were countless moments where decisions had to be made quickly. One such instance was during a sudden medical complication. The medical team was running around, and panic was setting in. I knew that I had to keep calm to make sound decisions. By focusing on my breathing, I was able to maintain clarity and assist the team effectively. This calmness allowed us to assess the situation objectively and take the necessary steps to stabilize him. Complex problems can feel overwhelming, especially under pressure. Breaking them down into smaller, more manageable parts can make them less daunting. This technique, known as "**chunking**," allows you to tackle one aspect of the problem at a time, leading to more effective solutions. In my coaching practice, I worked with a project manager who was overwhelmed by a massive project with tight deadlines. We broke down the project into smaller tasks and addressed each task individually. By focusing on these manageable chunks, she was able to make steady progress and complete the project successfully. This method not only improved her problem-solving skills but also reduced her stress levels. The **SCAMPER** technique is a creative problem-solving method that encourages thinking outside the box. SCAMPER stands for Substitute, Combine, Adapt, Modify, Put to another use, Eliminate, and Reverse. This approach helps generate innovative solutions by exploring different perspectives and possibilities. A client of mine, an entrepreneur, was struggling to differentiate his product in a saturated market. We applied the SCAMPER technique, which led to several creative ideas. By adapting and modifying existing features, and exploring how to put the product to new uses, he was able to create a unique value proposition that set his product apart. This not only solved his immediate problem but also positioned his business for long-term success. Having a **contingency plan** can significantly enhance problem-solving under pressure. It provides a backup plan, reducing the fear of failure and allowing for more confident decision-making. A well-thought-out contingency plan includes identifying potential risks and preparing alternative solutions in advance. When launching a new coaching program, we anticipated potential obstacles such as low enrollment and technical issues. By developing contingency plans for each scenario, we were able to address problems swiftly when they arose. This proactive approach not only ensured the program's success but also taught me the importance of being prepared for unexpected challenges. Incorporating **diverse perspectives** can enhance problem-solving by bringing in different viewpoints and ideas. Collaboration with individuals from various backgrounds and expertise can lead to more innovative and effective solutions. In a corporate training session, I facilitated a problem-solving workshop for a team facing a major product development issue. By encouraging team members from different departments to share their insights, we uncovered several novel solutions that the core team had not considered. This collaborative approach not only solved the immediate problem but also fostered a culture of teamwork and open communication. **Mental simulations** involve visualizing different scenarios and practicing responses to them. This technique helps prepare for high-pressure situations by mentally rehearsing various outcomes. Before important meetings or presentations, I often use brain simulations to anticipate potential questions and challenges. By visualizing the meeting and rehearsing my responses, I feel more prepared and confident. This technique has proven invaluable in high-stress environments where quick thinking is essential. **The 5 Whys technique** is a simple yet powerful tool for root cause analysis. By asking "why" five times, you can drill down to the underlying cause of a problem, leading to more effective solutions. A manufacturing client was experiencing frequent production delays. By applying the 5 Whys technique, we discovered that the root cause was a miscommunication between the supply chain and production departments. Addressing this communication gap resolved the delays and improved overall efficiency. This method has since become a staple in my problem-solving toolkit, helping clients uncover and address the true causes of their challenges. Encouraging a growth mindset fosters a willingness to tackle challenges head-on. In my own life, adopting a growth mindset has been transformative.

During Michael's recovery, there were setbacks and frustrations. However, by viewing each challenge as an opportunity to learn and grow, we remained motivated and persistent. This mindset not only improved our problem-solving abilities but also strengthened our overall adaptability. Solving skills under pressure requires a blend of inner strength, practical techniques, and a resilient mindset. By staying calm, breaking problems down, using creative methods like SCAMPER, developing contingency plans, leveraging diverse perspectives, practicing brain simulations, enhancing emotional intelligence, implementing the 5 Whys technique, and encouraging a growth mindset, we can effectively tackle high-pressure situations. These strategies, informed by personal experiences and insights from working with others, provide a robust toolkit for enhancing problem-solving skills and thriving under pressure. Through continuous practice and application, we can transform challenges into opportunities for growth and success.

Over the years, I have discovered and utilized various tools and ways that have significantly enhanced my ability to make quick and effective decisions. In this section, I will introduce some of these tools and share examples of how they have been applied successfully in my career. **SWOT Analysis** is a strategic planning tool that helps identify Strengths, Weaknesses, Opportunities, and Threats related to a decision. By categorizing these factors, you can gain a comprehensive understanding of the situation and make more informed decisions. Example: When I was considering expanding my coaching business to a new market, I used SWOT Analysis to evaluate the decision. By identifying our strengths (a strong brand reputation and a skilled team), weaknesses (limited knowledge of the new market), opportunities (a growing demand for coaching services), and threats (strong local competitors), I could develop a strategic plan that maximized our strengths and opportunities while mitigating weaknesses and threats. This analysis provided clarity and confidence in our decision to expand, leading to a successful market entry. **The RACI Matrix** is a responsibility assignment tool that clarifies roles and responsibilities in decision-making processes. RACI stands for Responsible, Accountable, Consulted, and Informed. By defining these roles, you can streamline decision-making and ensure that everyone knows their responsibilities. Example: In a project involving the launch of a new coaching program, we used the RACI Matrix to assign roles. I was responsible for developing the content (Responsible), my program director was accountable for the overall success of the launch (Accountable), our marketing team was consulted for promotional policies (Consulted), and our administrative staff was kept informed of progress (Informed). This clear delineation of roles ensured smooth coordination and efficient decision-making throughout the project, resulting in a successful launch. We previously mentioned the Matrix Analysis, also known as the **Pugh Method**, a technique used to evaluate and prioritize multiple options based on specific criteria. This tool helps in comparing different choices and selecting the best one objectively. Example: When deciding on a new software platform for managing client information, we used Decision Matrix Analysis. We identified key criteria such as cost, user-friendliness, features, and customer support. By scoring each software option against these criteria and weighting the importance of each criterion, we objectively determined the best choice. This structured approach not only saved time but also ensured that we selected the most suitable platform for our needs. **Paired Comparison Analysis** is a technique for ranking multiple options by comparing them in pairs. This method helps prioritize options when faced with several competing choices. Example: During a strategic planning session for my coaching business, we had to decide on the primary focus areas for the upcoming year. We used Paired Comparison Analysis to compare and rank different options such as expanding digital marketing, launching new programs, and increasing community engagement. By comparing each pair of options and scoring their relative importance, we were able to prioritize our focus areas effectively. This technique provided a clear direction and facilitated strategic decision-making. **Scenario Planning** involves creating detailed and plausible scenarios for the future to anticipate possible outcomes and make better decisions. This technique helps prepare for uncertainties and develop flexible outcomes. Example: When faced with the uncertainty of the COVID-19 pandemic, we used Scenario Planning to navigate its impact on our coaching business. We developed scenarios for various possibilities, such as prolonged lockdowns, partial reopenings, and complete recovery. For each scenario, we identified potential challenges and opportunities, and developed contingency plans. This proactive approach enabled us to adapt quickly to changing circumstances and continue serving our clients effectively, even during the most challenging times. **The Fishbone Diagram**, also known as the Ishikawa or Cause-and-Effect Diagram, is a tool used to identify the root causes of a problem. By visually mapping out the contributing factors, you can systematically analyze and address the underlying issues. Example: We used the Fishbone Diagram when faced with declining client satisfaction scores. By categorizing potential causes such as service quality, communication, scheduling, and training, we could identify the root issues. This analysis revealed that inadequate staff training was a significant factor. Addressing this root cause through enhanced training programs led to improved client satisfaction and better overall service quality. **Monte Carlo Simulation** is a statistical technique used to model the probability of different outcomes in a decision-making process. By running simulations, you can assess the risks and potential impacts of various decisions. Example: In a financial decision regarding a major investment in new technology, we used Monte Carlo Simulation to evaluate the potential risks and returns. By simulating different scenarios and their probabilities, we gained a clearer understanding of the potential financial impacts. This analysis helped us make a well-informed decision, balancing potential rewards with acceptable levels of risk. Efficient decision-making is crucial in navigating the complexities of today's world. Tools like SWOT Analysis, the RACI Matrix, Decision Matrix Analysis, Paired Comparison Analysis, Scenario Planning, the Fishbone Diagram, and Monte Carlo Simulation provide structured and systematic approaches to making informed decisions. By applying these tools and techniques in my career, I have been able to make more effective and confident decisions, leading to successful outcomes. Through continuous learning and adaptation, these tools can transform decision-making processes, enabling anyone to tackle challenges with clarity and precision.

In the whirlwind of today's world, mastering the art of efficient decision-making isn't just a skill—it's a superpower. From the battle-tested OODA Loop to the creative magic of rapid prototyping, each technique is a game-changer in its own right. Think about the OODA Loop—Observe, Orient, Decide, Act. It's not just a military strategy; it's a life hack for staying ahead of the curve. Picture this: you're navigating a crisis, everything's chaotic, and the pressure is sky-high. By observing the situation, orienting yourself to the information, deciding swiftly, and acting decisively, you're not just reacting—you're strategizing like a pro. This was my go-to approach during my brother Michael's recovery, turning what could have been a series of panicked decisions into a structured and effective action plan. Then there's the beauty of heuristics. These intellectual shortcuts, like the satisficing approach, save us from the rabbit hole of overthinking. In my coaching career, I've seen clients paralyzed by the pursuit of perfection. But when they embrace satisfaction—finding a solution that's good enough—they unlock the ability to move forward with confidence. It's about getting things done, not getting things perfect. Rapid prototyping adds a sprinkle of innovation to our decision-making toolkit. It's about testing, learning, and iterating at lightning speed. Imagine you're launching a new product. Instead of endless meetings and planning sessions, you develop a quick prototype, get feedback, and refine it. This approach not only speeds up the process but also grounds decisions in real-world data. It's a method that has saved me countless hours and helped turn ideas into successes more times than I can count. And let's not forget the simple genius of the Two-Minute Rule. Tackling tasks that take less than two minutes immediately clears the clutter from our to-do lists, freeing up mental space for the big decisions. It's a small habit with a huge impact, helping us stay focused and efficient. But efficient decision-making isn't just about tools and techniques—it's about mindset and culture. Fostering an environment where team members feel empowered to make decisions is crucial. When everyone knows their role and feels confident in their ability to contribute, decision-making becomes a shared, dynamic process. It's a culture shift that drives innovation and agility, turning good teams into great ones. So, what's the takeaway from all this? It's simple: efficient decision-making is your ticket to thriving in an unpredictable world. Whether you're a leader, an entrepreneur, or navigating personal challenges, you must equip yourself to make quick, confident, and effective decisions. Embrace structured frameworks like the OODA Loop and DECIDE model. Leverage the creative power of rapid prototyping. Apply practical methods like the Two-Minute Rule. Cultivate a supportive decision-making culture. And most importantly, keep learning and adapting. Remember, it's not just about making decisions faster—it's about making them better. As you integrate these into your life, you'll find that efficient decision-making isn't just a skill you use—it's a skill that transforms you, propelling you toward greater success. So go ahead, embrace these tools, make those decisions, and watch as you navigate life's challenges with newfound confidence and clarity. Here's to making smart, swift decisions and enjoying the journey along the way!

Continuous Excellence

Continuous excellence is the relentless pursuit of improvement, a mindset that values the process of becoming better over the mere attainment of goals. In a rapidly evolving world, where challenges and opportunities arise at an unprecedented pace, continuous excellence is not just a desirable trait—it's essential. It enables individuals and organizations to adapt, innovate, and thrive amidst constant change. By embracing continuous excellence, we ensure that we remain competitive, relevant, and resilient. The concept of continuous excellence goes beyond the traditional notions of success and achievement. It is about constantly seeking ways to enhance our skills, knowledge, and performance, no matter how successful we already are. This mindset fosters a culture of perpetual growth and development, where learning is a lifelong journey. Continuous excellence is about setting higher standards for ourselves and striving to meet and exceed them every day. It is a dynamic process that involves constant self-assessment, feedback integration, and adaptation. In today's digital age, technology plays a crucial role in facilitating continuous improvement. Modern technologies, such as artificial intelligence, data analytics, and wearable tech, provide us with unprecedented insights into our performance and areas for growth. For instance, wearable devices can track our physical activity, sleep patterns, and stress levels, offering real-time feedback and actionable data. AI-powered tools can analyze vast amounts of information to identify patterns and suggest improvements, whether in professional settings or personal endeavors. Feedback is another critical component of continuous excellence. It serves as a mirror, reflecting our strengths and areas needing improvement. Effective feedback mechanisms enable us to understand how our actions impact others and our overall performance. Whether it's through structured performance reviews, informal peer feedback, or self-reflection, integrating feedback allows us to make informed adjustments and refinements. In my own journey, feedback has been instrumental in driving my growth and success. Each piece of constructive criticism has been a stepping stone towards greater excellence. The combination of technology and feedback creates a powerful synergy for continuous improvement. Technology provides the tools and data needed to monitor progress, while feedback offers the qualitative insights that guide our development. Together, they form the backbone of a continuous improvement strategy, ensuring that we are always moving forward, learning, and evolving. As we delve deeper into this chapter, we will explore various modern technologies that aid continuous improvement and effective ways to integrate feedback into our routines. We will also draw on insights from leading experts and my own experiences to provide practical strategies for achieving continuous excellence. The journey towards continuous excellence is ongoing, and by embracing it, we can unlock our full potential and achieve extraordinary results.

As of now, staying ahead requires more than just hard work and determination—it demands the intelligent use of technology. Modern technologies like artificial intelligence (AI), data analytics, and wearable tech have revolutionized the way we approach continuous improvement. These tools offer valuable insights and practical solutions, enabling us to enhance our performance and efficiency systematically. AI has become a cornerstone in the quest for continuous improvement. Its ability to process and analyze vast amounts of data far surpasses human capabilities, allowing for more accurate predictions and personalized feedback. AI applications can range from simple chatbots that assist in daily tasks to sophisticated systems that optimize workflows and improve decision-making processes. For example, AI-powered personal assistants like Siri, Alexa, and Google Assistant can help manage schedules, set reminders, and even offer suggestions to improve productivity. In professional settings, AI tools such as IBM Watson can analyze data to provide actionable insights, identify trends, and predict outcomes, thus aiding in strategic planning and performance enhancement. AI can be integrated into daily routines through various apps and platforms. Tools like Grammarly use AI to enhance writing by providing real-time grammar and style suggestions, while fitness apps like MyFitnessPal offer personalized workout and nutrition plans based on individual goals and progress. Data analytics is another powerful technology driving continuous improvement. By examining large datasets, we can uncover patterns, correlations, and trends that inform better decision-making. In both personal and professional contexts, data analytics enables us to track performance, identify areas for improvement, and measure the impact of changes. For instance, in the workplace, platforms like Tableau and Power BI help visualize complex data, making it easier to understand and act upon. These tools can monitor key performance indicators (KPIs), track progress towards goals, and highlight inefficiencies that need addressing. For individual improvement, apps like Strava and Fitbit use data analytics to monitor physical activity, sleep patterns, and overall health, providing detailed reports and suggestions for improvement. Integrating data analytics into daily routines involves setting up systems to regularly collect and review data. For professionals, this could mean implementing a dashboard to monitor project progress and team performance. For individuals, it might involve using health tracking apps to gather data on daily activities and adjust habits accordingly. We mentioned it multiple times in the previous chapters, but wearable tech has made significant strides in recent years, offering innovative ways to monitor and improve our health and performance. Devices such as smartwatches, fitness trackers, and even smart clothing provide real-time feedback on various physical metrics, from heart rate and steps taken to sleep quality and stress levels. For example, devices like the Apple Watch or Fitbit not only track physical activity but also encourage healthy habits through reminders and motivational prompts. These wearables can sync with smartphones and computers to provide comprehensive reports and actionable insights. Athletes can use devices like the Whoop strap to monitor recovery and optimize training schedules based on physiological data. Integrating wearable tech into daily life is straightforward. By wearing these devices consistently and reviewing the data they collect, individuals can make informed decisions about their health and wellness. Setting specific goals within these apps, such as daily step counts or sleep targets, can help maintain motivation and focus. Some Real-Life Integration Examples I could tell you are these: a sales team might use an AI-powered CRM system like Salesforce Einstein to analyze customer interactions and sales data. The AI can identify successful strategies and recommend actions to improve future sales performance. By integrating this tool into their daily workflow, the team can continuously refine their approach based on real-time feedback. An individual aiming to improve their fitness might use a combination of MyFitnessPal and a Fitbit. MyFitnessPal can track nutritional intake while the Fitbit monitors physical activity. By analyzing the data from both sources, the individual can identify dietary patterns that impact performance and adjust their exercise regimen to optimize results. Someone managing a chronic condition like hypertension could use a smartwatch with built-in heart rate monitoring. The device can track heart rate throughout the day, alerting the user to any unusual spikes or dips. This data can be shared with a healthcare provider, enabling more accurate treatment adjustments and better overall management of the condition. A student using an AI-powered learning platform like Duolingo for language acquisition can benefit from personalized lesson plans that adapt based on their progress and performance. The AI can identify areas where the student struggles and provide targeted practice, enhancing the learning experience and ensuring continuous improvement.

As technology continues to evolve, its role in continuous improvement will only expand. Emerging technologies like virtual reality (VR) and augmented reality (AR) offer new ways to enhance learning and development. VR can simulate real-world scenarios for training purposes, while AR can overlay digital information onto the physical world, providing context-specific guidance. For example, a surgeon might use VR to practice complex procedures in a risk-free environment, honing their skills before performing the actual surgery. In everyday life, AR apps like Google Lens can provide real-time translations and information, aiding continuous learning and adaptation. Incorporating these technologies into our routines requires a mindset open to experimentation and adaptation. By staying informed about technological advancements and exploring how they can be applied to our personal and professional lives, we can ensure that we are always on the path to continuous excellence. Modern technologies like AI, data analytics, and wearable tech offer powerful tools for continuous improvement. By integrating these technologies into our daily routines, we can gain valuable insights, receive personalized feedback, and make informed decisions that drive our growth and performance. As we embrace these advancements, we unlock new potentials for excellence, ensuring that we are always evolving and improving in an ever-changing world.

Feedback is an essential component of continuous improvement. It serves as a mirror reflecting our actions and their impacts, enabling us to make informed adjustments that drive personal and professional growth. Whether it's through formal reviews, informal conversations, or self-reflection, feedback provides the insights needed to enhance performance, develop new skills, and achieve greater levels of excellence. Feedback is crucial for several reasons. First, it provides clarity. Often, we may not be fully aware of how our actions are perceived or the areas where we need improvement. Feedback brings these issues to light, offering a clear picture of our strengths and weaknesses. This awareness is the first step towards meaningful growth and development. Second, feedback fosters accountability. Knowing that our actions are being observed and evaluated encourages us to take responsibility for our performance. It motivates us to strive for better results and to continuously improve our skills and behaviors. Third, feedback drives motivation. Positive feedback reinforces good behavior, while constructive criticism provides the impetus to overcome challenges and improve. When delivered effectively, feedback can inspire us to push our boundaries and reach new heights. Finally, feedback supports learning and adaptation. In a rapidly changing world, the ability to adapt is crucial. Feedback helps us understand what works and what doesn't, enabling us to make necessary adjustments and stay on the path of continuous improvement. Gathering effective feedback requires intentionality and openness. Here are some methods to ensure you receive valuable and actionable insights: regular one-on-one meetings with mentors, managers, or peers provide opportunities for continuous feedback. These sessions should be informal, focused on specific areas of interest or concern, and conducted in a supportive environment. The 360-Degree Feedback method involves gathering feedback from a variety of sources, including peers, subordinates, and supervisors. It provides a comprehensive view of one's performance from different perspectives, highlighting areas of strength and opportunities for growth. Using structured surveys and questionnaires can help gather detailed feedback on specific topics. These tools can be anonymous, encouraging honest and candid responses. Numerous digital tools and platforms are available for collecting feedback. Apps like SurveyMonkey, Google Forms, and dedicated feedback platforms such as CultureAmp or Officevibe allow for efficient collection and analysis of feedback data. Regular self-assessment is a valuable feedback method. By taking time to reflect on your actions, decisions, and their outcomes, you can gain insights into your performance and identify areas for improvement. Mentors provide valuable feedback based on their experience and expertise. Regular interactions with a mentor can offer guidance, support, and constructive criticism, aiding in personal and professional growth.

Once feedback is gathered, the next step is to use it effectively. Here are some approaches to ensure that feedback drives continuous improvement: approach feedback with an open mind and a willingness to learn. Avoid becoming defensive or dismissive, and instead, view feedback as an opportunity for growth. Not all feedback will be equally valuable. Analyze the feedback you receive, identify common themes, and prioritize areas that need immediate attention. Focus on actionable insights that can lead to tangible improvements. Use the feedback to set clear, specific, and achievable goals. These goals should be aligned with your overall objectives and provide a roadmap for improvement. Create a detailed action plan outlining the steps needed to achieve your goals. This plan should include specific actions, timelines, and metrics for measuring progress. Take proactive steps to implement the changes identified in your action plan. This may involve acquiring new skills or changing behaviors. Continuous improvement is an ongoing process. After implementing changes, seek follow-up feedback to assess the effectiveness of your efforts and identify new areas for growth. Regularly reflect on your progress and make necessary adjustments to your action plan. This iterative process ensures that you remain on the path to continuous improvement.

In my own journey, feedback has been a critical driver of growth. I recall a period early in my career when I was leading a team through a particularly challenging project. Despite our efforts, we were struggling to meet our targets, and morale was low. I decided to conduct a 360-degree feedback session to understand the root of the issues. The feedback was eye-opening. My team felt that my communication style was too direct and that they lacked the autonomy to make decisions. This was a tough pill to swallow, but it was a necessary realization. I took this feedback to heart and worked on improving my leadership style. I started involving the team more in decision-making, encouraging open communication, and providing greater autonomy. The impact was profound. Team morale improved, and we started hitting our targets consistently. Another instance was during a personal fitness journey. I had plateaued in my progress and wasn't sure how to break through it. I sought feedback from a personal trainer who assessed my routine and diet. The feedback highlighted that my workouts lacked variety and that my diet wasn't aligned with my fitness goals. Implementing this feedback, I diversified my workouts and adjusted my diet, which helped me overcome the plateau and achieve new milestones. Feedback is a powerful tool for continuous improvement. It provides clarity, fosters accountability, drives motivation, and supports learning and adaptation. By effectively gathering and using feedback, we can make informed adjustments that lead to personal and professional growth. Through regular check-ins, 360-degree feedback, surveys, digital platforms, self-reflection, and mentorship, we can gather valuable insights. By being open, analyzing feedback, setting goals, developing action plans, implementing changes, seeking follow-up feedback, and reflecting on progress, we can ensure that feedback drives continuous improvement. Embracing feedback as a catalyst for growth has been instrumental in my journey, and it can be equally transformative for anyone committed to the pursuit of continuous excellence.

"Peak Performance," co-authored by Brad Stulberg and Steve Magness, offers a wealth of insights into achieving and maintaining high levels of performance. The book combines scientific research with practical advice, making it a valuable resource for anyone looking to improve continuously. Here, we'll summarize some key techniques from "Peak Performance" and relate them to the concept of continuous excellence. At the heart of "Peak Performance" is the Growth Equation: **Stress + Rest = Growth**. This simple formula encapsulates the idea that growth occurs when we push our limits (stress) and then allow ourselves to recover (rest). This balance is crucial for continuous improvement, as it prevents burnout and ensures sustainable progress.

Stress: This refers to any challenge that pushes us out of our comfort zone. It can be physical, psychical, or emotional. The key is to apply the right amount of stress—enough to stimulate growth but not so much that it leads to injury or burnout.

Rest: Equally important as stress, rest allows our bodies and minds to recover and adapt. This includes sleep, active recovery, and mental breaks. Rest is not merely the absence of activity but an essential component of the growth process.

Growth: The result of the stress-rest cycle is growth. Over time, our capacity to handle stress increases, leading to continuous improvement.

Relating this to continuous excellence, the Growth Equation underscores the importance of balancing effort with recovery. By managing this balance, we can maintain high performance over the long term, embodying the principle of continuous excellence. Periodization is another key concept from "Peak Performance." It involves structuring training or work into cycles of varying intensity. This method, commonly used in athletic training, can be applied to any area of performance.

Macrocycles: These are long-term cycles, often spanning several months or a year. They focus on overall goals and major phases of training or work.

Mesocycles: These intermediate cycles last several weeks to a few months. Each mesocycle targets specific aspects of performance, such as building strength, endurance, or skill.

Microcycles: The shortest cycles, usually lasting a week or so, focus on day-to-day training or work tasks.

Periodization allows for systematic planning and ensures that stress and rest are appropriately balanced throughout the year. For continuous excellence, this approach ensures that efforts are strategically aligned with goals, preventing overtraining and promoting sustained progress.

Stulberg and Magness highlight the importance of embracing stress as a catalyst for growth. This involves pushing beyond comfort zones and seeking out challenges that spur development. However, they caution against chronic stress, which can be detrimental.

Deliberate Practice: Engaging in deliberate practice involves focused, goal-oriented efforts to improve specific aspects of performance. This practice is demanding and requires concentration, but it is crucial for continuous improvement.

Adaptive Challenges: These are challenges that require adaptation and growth. By consistently seeking out and tackling adaptive challenges, we build capacity, driving continuous excellence.

In the context of continuous excellence, embracing stress means actively seeking opportunities to learn and grow. It involves a proactive approach to challenges, viewing them as opportunities rather than obstacles. Effective recovery is essential for balancing the stress-rest equation. "Peak Performance" emphasizes several methods: prioritizing quality sleep is fundamental. It is during sleep that the body and mind repair and consolidate learning. Light activities, such as walking or yoga, can aid recovery by promoting blood flow and reducing muscle stiffness. Taking regular breaks from intense cognitive work helps prevent burnout and maintains cognitive sharpness. Practices like meditation and deep breathing can reduce stress and enhance recovery. By incorporating these recovery schemes, we ensure that the periods of stress are complemented by adequate rest, leading to continuous improvement. Finally, "Peak Performance" highlights the importance of purpose and passion. Having a clear sense of purpose motivates sustained effort, while passion fuels the dedication needed for continuous improvement. Understanding the "why" behind our efforts provides direction and meaning, making it easier to persist through challenges. Passion drives intrinsic motivation, ensuring that the pursuit of excellence remains enjoyable and fulfilling. In the journey towards continuous excellence, purpose and passion serve as guiding stars. They keep us motivated and focused, helping us navigate the inevitable ups and downs of the improvement process. In conclusion, "Peak Performance" offers invaluable applications for continuous improvement, all of which align seamlessly with the concept of continuous excellence. The Growth Equation reminds us of the critical balance between stress and rest, while periodization provides a structured approach to managing efforts. Embracing stress for growth encourages us to seek out challenges, and effective recovery ensures that we can sustain high performance over time. Finally, purpose and passion keep us motivated and focused on our goals. By integrating these methods into our daily lives, we can achieve and maintain continuous excellence, consistently pushing the boundaries of our potential.

Continuous improvement has been a guiding principle throughout my life and career. Over the years, I've developed and refined a set of personal methods and strategies that have helped me push the boundaries of my potential. These modes are practical and adaptable, designed to fit into daily routines and drive sustained growth. Here, I share some of these unique methods and how they can be practically applied. One of the most powerful tools in my continuous improvement arsenal is the habit of daily reflection. Each evening, I spend about 15 minutes reviewing my day. I ask myself three key questions: What did I do well today? What could I have done better? What will I do differently tomorrow? This simple practice helps me identify areas of success and opportunities for improvement. By making small, incremental adjustments based on these reflections, I ensure that I'm continually evolving and enhancing my performance. Keeping a reflection journal where you answer these questions daily can be incredibly valuable. Over time, this journal will become a record of your progress and growth, helping you stay motivated and focused. Feedback is another crucial element in my approach to continuous improvement. I've developed a feedback integration system that ensures I don't just receive feedback but also use it to drive improvement. Regularly seeking feedback from trusted sources—mentors, colleagues, and self-assessments—is the first step. Then, I break down the feedback into specific, actionable items and develop a concrete action plan to address them. Implementing these changes and reviewing their impact after a set period allows me to assess their effectiveness and seek further feedback. This iterative process helps me stay on track and continually improve. Setting up monthly feedback sessions with mentors or peers and creating detailed action plans for each piece of significant feedback can ensure that feedback drives continuous improvement. Finding time for extensive learning can be challenging. To ensure continuous learning, I practice micro-learning—short, focused learning sessions that fit into daily schedules. These sessions typically last 10-15 minutes and cover a specific topic or skill. For example, setting a small learning goal for each day, such as reading an article, watching a tutorial, or practicing a new skill, can turn idle moments into productive ones. Educational apps like Duolingo, Coursera, or TED provide access to bite-sized learning content on the go, making it easier to integrate learning into your daily routine. Another method that has significantly impacted my continuous improvement journey is the 1% improvement rule. Inspired by the concept of marginal gains, I strive to improve by just 1% each day. This may seem insignificant, but over time, these small gains compound to produce significant results. Whether it's enhancing a skill, improving a process, or increasing efficiency, focusing on incremental improvements ensures continuous progress. Identifying one small area for improvement each day and working on it can lead to substantial growth over time. Keeping a log of these daily improvements helps visualize your growth and stay motivated. Perseverance is a key component of continuous excellence. To enhance focus, reduce stress, and improve inner clarity, I incorporate mindfulness practices into my daily routine. Techniques such as meditation, deep breathing exercises, and visualization help me maintain a positive mindset and stay centered. Using meditation apps like Headspace or Calm can guide daily meditation sessions, while practicing deep breathing exercises during breaks can help relax and refocus. Visualization, where you spend a few minutes each day visualizing success in upcoming tasks or challenges, reinforces a positive outlook and prepares you for success. Finally, conducting post-mortem analyses after completing any significant project or task has been invaluable. This structured review helps evaluate what went well and what didn't, identifying lessons learned and areas for improvement. By discussing successes, challenges, and lessons learned after each project, you can create a knowledge base that informs future projects and ensures continuous growth. These personal methods for continuous improvement—daily reflection, feedback integration, micro-learning, the 1% improvement rule, mindfulness, and project post-mortems—have been instrumental in my journey towards continuous excellence. They are practical, adaptable, and designed to fit seamlessly into daily routines. By incorporating these strategies into your own life, you can foster a mindset of perpetual growth and consistently push the boundaries of your potential. Remember, the path to continuous excellence is not about making giant leaps but taking consistent, incremental steps every day.

The principles from Seth Godin's "The Practice" offer a profound framework for maintaining and enhancing continuous excellence. "The Practice" emphasizes the importance of consistent effort and dedication to craft, which aligns seamlessly with the pursuit of continuous excellence. This approach is less about seeking perfection and more about embracing the process of ongoing improvement through regular practice and perseverance. One of the central tenets of "The Practice" is the concept of showing up every day. Excellence is not achieved overnight; it is the result of consistent, incremental progress. By committing to daily practice, whether it's honing a skill, working on a project, or developing new habits, we create a steady rhythm that fosters growth. This regularity helps to build momentum, making it easier to sustain long-term efforts and avoid burnout. The act of showing up consistently, even when motivation wanes, underscores the importance of persistence in achieving continuous excellence. Consistency is critical because it creates a reliable foundation for progress. Regular practice enables us to refine our skills and deepen our understanding over time. For instance, a writer who commits to writing a few hundred words every day will see significant improvement over months and years. Similarly, an athlete who trains consistently, even on days when they feel less motivated, will build the physical and grit needed for peak performance. In my own journey, the habit of daily reflection and setting small, manageable goals has been vital. These consistent efforts accumulate, leading to substantial improvements over time. Another key idea from "The Practice" is the focus on the process rather than the outcome. This shift in mindset encourages us to find satisfaction and motivation in the act of doing, rather than being solely fixated on the end result. By valuing the process, we can maintain enthusiasm and drive, even when progress seems slow. This perspective helps to mitigate the frustration that can come from setting overly ambitious goals and not meeting them immediately. Embracing the process allows for a more sustainable approach to growth, one that can be maintained over the long haul. Persistence is equally essential in the pursuit of continuous excellence. It involves maintaining effort and commitment, even in the face of challenges and setbacks. Persistence means pushing through difficulties, learning from failures, and continuing to strive towards improvement. This is what ultimately leads to breakthroughs and significant achievements. Godin's emphasis on the practice of persistence—repeatedly engaging in our craft and pushing our limits—reinforces the notion that continuous excellence is a journey marked by ongoing effort and adaptation. Moreover, "The Practice" highlights the importance of seeking feedback and being open to change. Regularly soliciting feedback helps to identify areas for improvement and ensures that we are on the right path. This openness to external insights complements the internal consistency of showing up daily. By integrating feedback into our practice, we can make informed adjustments that enhance our growth trajectory. In applying the ideas from "The Practice" to maintain and enhance continuous excellence, it's clear that the foundation lies in consistent effort and unwavering persistence. These principles foster a mindset that values progress over perfection, encourages steadfastness in the face of challenges, and embraces ongoing improvement as a lifelong endeavor. By showing up every day, focusing on the practice itself, and remaining open to feedback, we can sustain the drive for excellence and continually push the boundaries of our potential.

Embracing continuous improvement is a powerful catalyst for personal and professional growth. By integrating strategies such as daily reflection, feedback integration, micro-learning, the 1% improvement rule, mindfulness, and structured reviews into your daily routine, you can foster a mindset of perpetual growth and excellence. These techniques are designed to be practical and adaptable, ensuring they fit seamlessly into your life, no matter how busy it might be. Remember, the journey towards continuous excellence is not about making giant leaps overnight but about taking consistent, incremental steps every day. Show up, embrace the process, and be persistent in your efforts. Value the progress you make, however small, and keep pushing your boundaries. As you implement these, you'll find yourself evolving, adapting, and reaching new heights. The principles of "The Practice" remind us that excellence is a journey, not a destination. By committing to this journey, you can unlock your full potential and achieve extraordinary results. Start today, and let the path of continuous improvement lead you to a future filled with success and fulfillment.

Part IV: Advanced Strategies and Practical Applications

Facing and Overcoming Failure

Failures are inevitable in our rapidly evolving world, where technological advancements and social dynamics constantly challenge us. Whether it's a setback in our professional lives, personal disappointments, or unforeseen accidents, how we respond to these failures defines our journey. This chapter delves into modern failures and how to remain steadfast and high-performing despite them. A few years ago, I faced a significant professional setback that tested me like never before. I had poured my heart and soul into a startup project, investing countless hours and resources. It was a venture I believed would revolutionize our industry. However, despite all the hard work, the project failed spectacularly. The product launch was marred by technical glitches, and negative reviews flooded in. Our investors pulled out, and the team I had built with such care began to disband. This failure felt like a personal and professional disaster. The sense of loss and disappointment was overwhelming. I questioned my abilities and wondered if I would ever recover from such a blow. It was during this challenging time that I had to dig deep and find the force to move forward. Modern failures are not just about personal or professional setbacks. They encompass a wide array of challenges brought about by new technologies and shifting societal norms. From cybersecurity breaches to public scrutiny on social media, the nature of failure has evolved. These failures require a new set of skills to navigate effectively. Talking about failure is crucial for several reasons. First, it normalizes the experience of failure, reducing the stigma and shame often associated with it. By openly discussing our failures, we acknowledge that everyone encounters setbacks, which fosters a more supportive and understanding environment. Second, sharing stories of failure provides valuable learning opportunities. When we talk about what went wrong and how we responded, we offer insights that others can use to navigate similar challenges. These lessons can prevent others from making the same mistakes and help them recover more quickly when they do encounter failure. Finally, discussing failure promotes well-being and balance. It helps us build a mindset that views failure not as a final defeat but as a temporary setback and a stepping stone to success. This shift in perspective encourages perseverance and continuous improvement, essential qualities for achieving long-term success. By addressing failure openly and constructively, we empower ourselves and others to embrace challenges, learn from mistakes, and continue striving toward our goals. This chapter aims to equip you with the tools to face modern failures with determination.

Modern technological and social challenges have introduced new types of failures that can have far-reaching impacts on our personal and professional lives. Unlike the simpler times where failures were confined to specific domains, today's failures can ripple across various aspects of life due to the pervasive nature of technology and social media. One of the most significant technological challenges we face today is the threat of **cybersecurity breaches**. With the increasing reliance on digital platforms for business operations, personal communication, and data storage, the risk of cyber-attacks has escalated. Hackers are constantly evolving their tactics, making it difficult for individuals and organizations to safeguard their information. A single breach can lead to the loss of sensitive data, financial setbacks, and a damaged reputation, illustrating the modern complexity of technological failures. Social media, another cornerstone of modern life, presents its unique set of challenges. While it offers incredible opportunities for connection and communication, it also exposes individuals and businesses to the potential for social backlash. A single **misstep or controversial** post can go viral, resulting in public scrutiny, harassment, and even boycotts. The speed at which information spreads on social media amplifies the impact of these failures, making it harder to manage and recover from them. One stark example of a modern technological failure is the cybersecurity breach. Consider the 2017 Equifax data breach, where hackers accessed the personal information of approximately 147 million people. This incident not only caused significant financial losses for the company but also exposed millions to the risk of identity theft. The fallout from such breaches can be long-lasting, affecting consumer trust and organizational stability. And if we are talking social media, take the case of a major corporation that posted an ill-conceived advertisement on a popular platform. The ad was quickly deemed insensitive by the public, leading to widespread criticism and calls for boycotts. The speed and scale of the backlash were overwhelming, causing a substantial drop in the company's stock price and forcing them to issue multiple public apologies. This example highlights how quickly a situation can spiral out of control in the digital age. In my career, I have faced several instances where modern technological challenges tested my patience. A notable example occurred a few years ago when I was leading a project that involved developing a new software platform for a client. Despite our best efforts to implement robust security measures, we experienced a cybersecurity breach. Hackers infiltrated our system, compromising sensitive client information and disrupting our operations. The immediate aftermath was chaotic. We had to inform the client, manage the fallout, and work tirelessly to secure our system. This experience was a harsh reminder of the vulnerabilities inherent in today's digital world. It forced me to reevaluate our security protocols and invest more heavily in cybersecurity measures. The road to recovery was challenging, but it also provided valuable lessons. We learned the importance of having contingency plans, the need for constant vigilance, and the value of transparent communication during crises. Another personal anecdote involves facing a social media backlash. As a public figure and author, I have had my share of controversial opinions. On one occasion, a comment I made during an interview was taken out of context and spread widely on social media. Within hours, I was inundated with negative comments and messages. The backlash was intense, and for a moment, I felt overwhelmed by the sheer volume of criticism. Navigating this storm required strategic thinking. I had to clarify my stance and issue a well-thought-out public statement to address the misunderstanding.

More importantly, I had to maintain my composure and not let the negativity affect my mental health. This experience reinforced the need for peace in the face of public scrutiny and the importance of effective communication in mitigating the damage. Through these experiences, I have come to appreciate the critical role of elasticity in overcoming modern failures. Each failure, whether technological or social, offers a unique set of challenges that require a strategic and composed response. Learning from these failures has enabled me to develop more robust systems and strategies to prevent similar issues in the future. For instance, after the cybersecurity breach, I implemented a series of measures to enhance our digital security. We conducted thorough security audits, updated our protocols, and provided extensive training to our team on recognizing and responding to potential threats. These steps not only strengthened our security but also fostered a culture of vigilance and preparedness. Similarly, my experience with social media backlash taught me the importance of careful communication and reputation management. I now approach public statements and social media interactions with greater caution and thoughtfulness, understanding the potential ramifications of my words. I have also learned to engage with criticism constructively, using it as an opportunity for growth and improvement.

It involves cultivating a mindset that views failures as opportunities for growth rather than definitive setbacks. This process requires emotional strength, willpower, and the ability to adapt to changing circumstances. Failure is an inevitable part of life and growth.

Embracing failure means acknowledging it without letting it define you. Each failure carries lessons that can guide future actions and decisions. For instance, if a project doesn't succeed, analyze what went wrong, identify areas for improvement, and apply those lessons to your next endeavor. This mindset shift from seeing failure as a negative outcome to viewing it as a valuable learning experience is crucial. By focusing on what you can learn rather than what you lost, you maintain a positive outlook and stay motivated to keep moving forward. No one succeeds alone. A resilient person understands the importance of a support network that includes friends, family, mentors, and colleagues. These individuals provide guidance, encouragement, and constructive feedback, helping you navigate the emotional challenges of failure. When facing setbacks, having people who believe in you and offer different perspectives can make a significant difference. A strong support system can keep you grounded, provide emotional stability, and offer practical advice during tough times. Resilience is not solely about determination; it also involves taking care of your physical and emotional well-being. Self-care practices reduce stress, improve mood, and enhance overall health, which are its essential components. When you prioritize self-care, you build a solid foundation that supports your ability to handle adversity. The modern world is constantly changing, and flexibility is key to this. Staying adaptable means being open to new ideas and willing to adjust yourself as needed. Whether it's a shift in market trends, technological advancements, or personal circumstances, adaptability allows you to respond effectively to unexpected challenges and seize new opportunities. **Embracing change** rather than resisting it enables you to remain proactive and resourceful in the face of uncertainty. Setting achievable goals is a powerful way to build it. Realistic goals provide a clear sense of direction and purpose, helping you stay focused and motivated. Break down larger objectives into smaller, manageable tasks, and celebrate your progress along the way. This approach prevents overwhelm and maintains momentum, allowing you to tackle challenges systematically. When setbacks occur, realistic goals help you maintain perspective and keep striving toward your objectives. Talking about failure is crucial for several reasons. First, it normalizes the experience of failure, reducing the stigma and shame often associated with it. By openly discussing our failures, we acknowledge that everyone encounters setbacks, which fosters a more supportive and understanding environment. Second, sharing stories of failure provides valuable learning opportunities. When we talk about what went wrong and how we responded, we offer insights that others can use to navigate similar challenges. These lessons can prevent others from making the same mistakes and help them recover more quickly when they do encounter failure. Finally, **discussing failure**. It helps us build a mindset that views failure not as a final defeat but as a temporary setback and a stepping stone to success. This shift in perspective encourages perseverance and continuous improvement, essential qualities for achieving long-term success. Building toughness is a continuous process that involves embracing failure, developing a support system, practicing self-care, staying adaptable, and setting realistic goals. By implementing these, you can cultivate the strength needed to face modern failures with confidence and determination. The journey may be challenging, but each step forward brings you closer to success and personal growth. It's not just about bouncing back but thriving in the face of adversity. Let's explore some practical programs to help you remain resilient and perform at your best, even when faced with setbacks, drawing from my own experiences and techniques I've developed over the years. Reframing your mindset is a foundational strategy. This approach involves changing how you perceive and respond to setbacks, shifting from a defeatist attitude to one that views failure as an opportunity for growth and learning. Here's how you can effectively reframe your mindset: the first step in reframing your mindset is to understand that failure is an integral part of the journey to success. Every successful individual or organization has encountered numerous failures along the way. These setbacks are not roadblocks but stepping stones that provide valuable lessons and insights. Recognizing this reality can help you embrace failure rather than fear it. When my startup project failed, it felt like the end of the world. I had invested countless hours and resources, and seeing it collapse was devastating. However, by reminding myself that failure is a natural part of any ambitious endeavor, I began to accept it as a learning experience rather than a personal catastrophe. A fixed mindset is one where individuals believe their abilities and intelligence are static and unchangeable. In contrast, a growth mindset is the belief that abilities and intelligence can be developed through dedication, hard work, and learning. Embracing a growth mindset is crucial because it encourages you to see failures as opportunities to develop and improve. For example, instead of thinking, "I failed because I'm not good enough," reframe your thoughts to, "I failed, but I can learn from this and improve." This shift in perspective transforms how you view your abilities and potential. Each failure carries within it a wealth of knowledge. Embracing failure as a learning opportunity means actively seeking out the lessons it offers. After experiencing a setback, take time to reflect on what happened, why it happened, and what you can learn from it. In today's rapidly changing professional landscape, effectively handling failures is crucial for both personal and organizational success. Modern professional challenges, such as remote work dynamics, adapting to rapid technological changes, and maintaining work-life balance, present unique hurdles that require innovative schemes and a well-researched approach. The shift to remote work has revolutionized the way we operate, offering flexibility but also introducing issues like isolation, miscommunication, and decreased productivity. Research over the past five years has highlighted several strategies to mitigate these challenges. A study by Buffer (2020) revealed that 20% of remote workers struggle with loneliness, while another 20% face difficulties with collaboration and communication. To address these issues, enhancing communication is vital. Utilizing various communication tools, such as video conferencing, instant messaging, and collaborative platforms, helps bridge the gap created by physical distance. Regular virtual meetings and check-ins ensure that team members stay connected and aligned. Moreover, fostering team cohesion is essential. Remote work can lead to a sense of isolation among team members. Research by Harvard Business Review (2018) suggests that virtual team-building activities and informal chat sessions significantly enhance team cohesion and foster a sense of community and belonging. Creating opportunities for social interaction helps mitigate the feeling of isolation. Implementing clear work processes is another critical strategy. Establishing workflows, roles, and responsibilities ensures that everyone knows what is expected of them. A study by McKinsey & Company (2020) found that companies using project management tools to track progress and manage tasks saw a 25% increase in productivity. These tools enhance productivity and accountability, making remote work more efficient. Technological advancements are evolving at an unprecedented pace, posing a significant challenge for professionals trying to keep up. Failing to adapt can lead to obsolescence and missed opportunities. Continuous learning and embracing innovation are key points to navigate these changes. Promoting continuous learning is essential. Encouraging a culture of continuous learning ensures that employees stay updated with the latest technological trends and advancements. Research by Deloitte (2019) indicates that organizations investing in continuous learning see a 37% higher employee engagement rate and a 21% increase in profitability. Providing access to online courses, workshops, and training programs can help bridge knowledge gaps and keep employees current. Encouraging innovation is equally important. Creating an environment that fosters innovation encourages employees to experiment with new ideas and technologies. A report by PwC (2019) found that companies with a strong innovation culture are 27% more likely to be market leaders. This environment can lead to the development of new solutions and improvements in existing processes. Leveraging cross-functional teams can also facilitate innovation. By bringing together diverse perspectives and expertise, cross-functional teams can develop innovative solutions to technological challenges. A study by the Boston Consulting Group (2018) found that diverse teams produce 19% more revenue from innovation compared to less diverse teams. The digital era has blurred the lines between work and personal life, leading to burnout and decreased job satisfaction. Balancing these aspects is critical to maintaining overall well-being and productivity. Research by the World Health Organization (2019) highlights that burnout is a major issue, with long working hours and constant connectivity being significant contributors. Implementing boundaries between work and personal life is crucial. Encouraging employees to set specific working hours and take regular breaks can help maintain a healthy work-life balance. A study by Stanford University (2017) found that productivity declines sharply after 50 hours per week, underscoring the importance of maintaining reasonable working hours. Promoting mental health and well-being is another essential strategy. Providing resources such as counseling services, mental health days, and wellness programs can support employees in managing stress and maintaining their well-being. The American Psychological Association (2020) reports that employees with access to psychological resources are more productive and have higher job satisfaction. Flexible working arrangements can also contribute to a better work-life balance. Allowing employees to choose their working hours or work from different locations can reduce stress and increase job satisfaction. A study by the International Labour Organization (2019) found that flexible work arrangements can improve work-life balance, reduce stress, and enhance productivity. In conclusion, handling modern failures requires a proactive and strategic approach, supported by the latest research. Whether dealing with remote work challenges, adapting to technological advancements, or maintaining work-life balance, addressing these issues constructively and strategically is essential. By embracing continuous learning, fostering innovation, and promoting well-being, individuals and organizations can navigate these challenges for future success.

Throughout this chapter, we've explored the intricacies of handling modern failures in a rapidly evolving professional landscape. We delved into the challenges posed by remote work dynamics, the necessity of adapting to technological advancements, and the critical importance of maintaining a work-life balance in the digital era. Each of these areas presents unique hurdles, but with strategic approaches and a resilient mindset, these challenges can be navigated effectively. First, we discussed the challenges of remote work. As the global workforce increasingly moves toward remote and hybrid models, issues like isolation, miscommunication, and decreased productivity have become prominent. Research underscores the importance of enhancing communication through various tools, fostering team cohesion with virtual team-building activities, and implementing clear work processes. These plans not only bridge the physical distance but also enhance productivity and team morale. Second, we addressed the rapid pace of technological change. Continuous learning and embracing innovation are crucial to keep pace with these changes. Promoting a culture of continuous learning ensures that employees remain updated on the latest trends and advancements. Encouraging innovation within the workplace can lead to the development of new solutions and improve existing processes. Leveraging cross-functional teams can bring diverse perspectives and expertise, driving innovation and staying ahead of the curve. Third, we explored the importance of maintaining a work-life balance. The blurring lines between work and personal life can lead to burnout and decreased job satisfaction. Implementing boundaries, promoting mental health and well-being, and offering flexible working arrangements are essential to maintain a healthy balance. These measures help reduce stress, increase job satisfaction, and enhance overall productivity. This is the bedrock of overcoming modern failures. It's not just about bouncing back from setbacks but growing stronger through the process. It enables individuals to navigate the complexities of modern professional challenges with grace and determination. It involves reframing failures as learning opportunities, leveraging support networks, prioritizing self-care, and maintaining a forward-looking perspective. In the face of remote work challenges, flexibility means adapting communication strategies and fostering a sense of community despite physical distance. When dealing with technological advancements, it involves continuously learning and embracing innovation, seeing every challenge as an opportunity to grow and improve. For work-life balance, it is about setting boundaries and prioritizing well-being to sustain long-term productivity and job satisfaction. As we navigate this complex and modern world, it's essential to remember that every failure is a stepping stone to success. The plans discussed in this chapter are tools to help you handle modern failures constructively. Remember, these are not traits you're born with; but rather skills that can be developed and strengthened over time. Embrace challenges as opportunities for growth. Surround yourself with a strong support network and never underestimate the power of continuous learning. Stay adaptable and open to change, and most importantly, prioritize your well-being. By adopting these, you can turn setbacks into setups for a stronger, more resilient future. Failures are inevitable, but how you respond to them defines your path. Cultivate this, and let every failure be a lesson that propels you forward. The journey may be challenging, but remember that every single step brings you closer to your goals and aspirations. Stay determined, stay resilient, and remember that your greatest successes often come from your hardest challenges.

Enhancing Creativity and Innovation

Innovation is the lifeblood of progress, particularly in an era marked by rapid technological advancements, global interconnectedness, and unprecedented challenges. As we navigate this dynamic landscape, creativity emerges as a critical asset, enabling us to tackle problems and seize opportunities in ways that were previously unimaginable. The pace of technological change is staggering. Innovations such as artificial intelligence, blockchain, and biotechnology are transforming industries at an unprecedented rate. Creativity is essential in this context because it enables individuals and organizations to not only keep up with these changes but also to leverage them for competitive advantage. For instance, AI is revolutionizing fields ranging from healthcare to finance. Creative applications of AI include predictive analytics for personalized medicine, algorithms for detecting fraudulent transactions, and AI-driven customer service bots that enhance user experience. Companies that harness creativity to integrate AI into their operations are not just keeping up—they are leading the way. Moreover, the tech industry itself thrives on creative innovation. Startups are constantly pushing the boundaries of what's possible, from developing cutting-edge software solutions to pioneering new hardware technologies. The ability to think creatively and envision future possibilities is what drives the industry forward and keeps it evolving at such a rapid pace.

Economic landscapes are increasingly volatile, with frequent shifts caused by global events, market dynamics, and policy changes. Creativity allows businesses to be agile and resilient in the face of such uncertainty. Innovative financial strategies, like crowdfunding, peer-to-peer lending, and cryptocurrencies, have emerged as creative solutions to traditional funding challenges. Startups, for example, often face funding constraints. Creative approaches such as equity crowdfunding enable them to raise capital by engaging a broad base of investors. This not only provides financial resources but also builds a community of supporters and potential customers. During economic downturns, businesses that can pivot creatively often find new avenues for growth. For instance, during the 2008 financial crisis, many companies turned to digital transformation as a way to cut costs and increase efficiency. This creative adaptation not only helped them survive the downturn but also positioned them for greater success in the recovery period. Society faces significant challenges, including climate change, social inequality, and public health crises. Traditional methods of addressing these issues are often insufficient. Creativity fosters the development of novel solutions that can have a profound impact. One example is the use of technology to improve access to clean water. Innovative solutions like solar-powered water purification systems and atmospheric water generators are providing clean drinking water in areas where conventional methods are not feasible. These creative solutions are saving lives and improving health outcomes in many parts of the world. In the realm of social innovation, creative approaches are transforming education and healthcare. Programs like Khan Academy and Coursera are democratizing education by providing free or low-cost access to high-quality courses. Telemedicine platforms are making healthcare accessible to remote and underserved populations. These innovations are reducing barriers and creating opportunities for millions of people. Environmental challenges, particularly climate change, require a high degree of creativity to address. Solutions such as renewable energy technologies, carbon capture and storage, and sustainable agriculture practices are the result of innovative thinking. Creative approaches to urban planning, like the development of green cities and smart grids, are also essential for building sustainable communities. In the business world, creativity is a key differentiator. It drives the development of unique products, services, and customer experiences that set companies apart from their competitors. Creative companies are better equipped to meet changing consumer demands and to anticipate market trends. Apple, for example, is renowned for its creativity in product design and user experience. The company's ability to blend technology with aesthetics and functionality has made its products highly desirable. Apple's approach to innovation goes beyond the products themselves, extending to retail experiences, marketing strategies, and customer service. Companies that encourage creativity in their workforce often see higher levels of employee engagement and satisfaction. Creative employees are more likely to come up with innovative solutions to problems, improving the overall efficiency and effectiveness of the organization. This not only leads to better business outcomes but also fosters a positive work environment. Creativity is not limited to organizational success; it is also crucial for personal and professional development. In an increasingly complex and dynamic world, individuals need to be able to think creatively to solve problems, make decisions, and adapt to new situations. Creative thinking enhances problem-solving skills by enabling individuals to see problems from different angles and to devise unconventional solutions. It also fosters continuous learning and growth, as creative individuals are more likely to seek out new experiences, knowledge, and skills. In the professional realm, creativity can lead to career advancement and job satisfaction. Creative professionals are often more engaged and fulfilled in their work, as they are able to express themselves and contribute meaningfully to their organizations. Moreover, employers highly value creativity, recognizing it as a critical skill for innovation and competitiveness. For example, individuals who pursue creative hobbies such as writing, painting, or music often develop a greater capacity for creative thinking in their professional lives. These activities can enhance cognitive flexibility, improve emotional intelligence, and provide a healthy outlet for stress, all of which contribute to overall well-being and productivity. In a crowded marketplace, creativity is essential for developing unique products and services that stand out from the competition. Companies that foster a culture of innovation are better equipped to anticipate and respond to customer needs, leading to products and services that not only meet but exceed expectations. For example, Dyson revolutionized the household appliance market with its innovative vacuum technology. By rethinking the conventional design and functionality of vacuum cleaners, Dyson created a product that was not only more efficient but also more aesthetically appealing. This creative approach allowed Dyson to carve out a niche in a highly competitive market. Creativity also plays a crucial role in enhancing the customer experience. Businesses that prioritize creative thinking are able to design customer journeys that are engaging, seamless, and memorable. This can include everything from intuitive product interfaces to personalized customer service and innovative loyalty programs. Consider how Disney has used creativity to enhance the customer experience at its theme parks. From immersive attractions and themed environments to interactive technologies and personalized services, Disney's creative approach ensures that visitors have a magical and unforgettable experience. This not only drives repeat visits but also fosters strong brand loyalty. Creative marketing and branding are vital for capturing the attention of consumers and differentiating a brand in the marketplace. Companies that leverage creativity in their marketing strategies are able to create compelling campaigns that resonate with their target audience and drive engagement. Nike's "Just Do It" campaign is a prime example of creative marketing. By tapping into the universal appeal of motivation and perseverance, Nike created a powerful and enduring brand message. The campaign's success lies in its simplicity, emotional resonance, and ability to inspire action, making it one of the most iconic ones of all time. A company's ability to maintain a competitive edge often depends on its internal culture. Organizations that encourage creativity and innovation at all levels are more likely to develop breakthrough ideas and maintain a dynamic, forward-thinking environment. This involves fostering an open-minded atmosphere where employees feel empowered to experiment, take risks, and share their ideas. Google's approach to fostering an innovative culture includes initiatives like "20% time," where employees are encouraged to spend 20% of their work hours on projects, they are passionate about. This policy has led to the development of several successful products, including Gmail and Google Maps, demonstrating how a culture that values creativity can drive significant innovation. Creativity enables businesses to be agile and responsive to market changes. In rapidly evolving industries, the ability to pivot and adapt creatively is crucial for long-term success. This involves not only responding to emerging trends but also anticipating future developments and positioning the company accordingly. For instance, Netflix transitioned from a DVD rental service to a streaming platform, and eventually into content production. This creative pivot allowed Netflix to stay ahead of the curve and dominate the entertainment industry. By continuously innovating and adapting to changing market dynamics, Netflix has maintained its competitive edge and continued to grow its subscriber base. On a personal note, creativity played a crucial role in my brother Michael's recovery journey. After his accident, traditional rehabilitation methods weren't yielding the desired results. It was through creative thinking and innovative approaches that we discovered new therapies and technologies that significantly improved his condition. For example, we had already talked about how incorporating virtual reality (VR) into his physical therapy regimen provided a stimulating and engaging way for him to perform exercises. VR not only made the therapy sessions more enjoyable but also enhanced his motor skills and cognitive functions. This experience reinforced my belief in the power of creativity to overcome even the most daunting challenges. Modern challenges require modern solutions. Economic volatility, climate change, and social inequalities are complex issues that demand creative approaches. For instance, in the face of climate change, innovators are developing renewable energy technologies, sustainable agriculture practices, and circular economy models. These creative solutions are not only addressing environmental issues but are also creating new economic opportunities and improving quality of life. In the realm of social innovation, creativity is driving progress in areas such as education, healthcare, and community development. Programs that use technology to provide remote education, telemedicine services to reach underserved populations, and social enterprises that empower marginalized communities are just a few examples of how innovative thinking is making a difference. Creativity is more than just a buzzword; it is an essential skill for navigating and thriving in the modern world. By embracing innovative thinking, we can address complex challenges, drive progress, and unlock new opportunities. Whether it's in business, healthcare, social development, or personal growth, creativity empowers us to envision and create a better future. As we move forward in this chapter, we'll explore practical techniques to cultivate and apply innovation, ensuring that you have the tools to harness your creative potential and make a meaningful impact in your field.

Innovation is not just a stroke of genius or a sudden burst of inspiration; it is often the result of deliberate practices and a mindset that fosters creative thinking. In this section, we'll explore practical methods to develop a creative mindset, discuss daily habits and practices that encourage innovation, and share personal anecdotes of how these ones have been successfully applied. Developing a creative mindset is crucial in today's rapidly changing world, as it equips individuals with the ability to think innovatively and solve complex problems. One of the key components of a creative mindset is embracing curiosity and continuous learning. Curiosity drives exploration and the pursuit of new knowledge, which are essential for generating fresh ideas. By maintaining a curious mindset, individuals can explore diverse topics, ask insightful questions, and seek new experiences. This continuous learning process ensures that the mind remains sharp and receptive to new ideas. Engaging with online courses, attending workshops, and participating in discussions with people from different fields are excellent ways to foster curiosity and continuous learning. Challenging assumptions and embracing failure are also fundamental to developing a creative mindset. Creativity thrives when individuals question the status quo and explore new possibilities. By regularly **challenging assumptions**, one can uncover hidden opportunities and develop innovative solutions. Embracing failure is equally important, as it is an inherent part of the creative process. As we thoroughly discussed in the previous chapter, each failure provides valuable lessons and insights that bring individuals closer to success. **Cultivating resilience** and maintaining a positive attitude towards failure can significantly enhance one's ability to think creatively. Reflection, through activities like **journaling**, allows individuals to process their thoughts and experiences, leading to the generation of new ideas. By regularly taking time to reflect, individuals can better understand their creative processes and identify areas for improvement. Developing a creative mindset involves embracing **curiosity**, challenging assumptions, and practicing mindfulness and reflection. These practices not only enhance one's ability to think innovatively but also equip individuals with the skills necessary to navigate and thrive in a complex, dynamic world. Fostering innovative thinking is not a one-time effort but a continuous process that can be nurtured through daily habits and practices. Creating a **stimulating environment** is one of the foundational steps. Your physical space significantly impacts your ability to think creatively. Surround yourself with items that inspire you, such as books, artwork, and plants. Designate a specific area for creative work that is free from distractions. Regularly changing your environment can also spark new ideas. Working in different locations, like a coffee shop, park, or another room, can stimulate your mind and break the monotony of routine. Engaging in creative exercises daily can significantly boost your innovative thinking. Brainstorming sessions are effective in generating a plethora of ideas in a short time. Set aside time regularly for brainstorming, either alone or with a group, and aim for quantity over quality initially to allow free-flowing creativity. **Mind mapping** is another powerful tool that helps in organizing thoughts and exploring connections between ideas. Start with a central concept and branch out to related ideas, allowing your thoughts to flow freely. Divergent thinking exercises, such as brainstorming multiple uses for a common object, encourage you to think in various directions and consider multiple possibilities. Cultivating diverse interests and hobbies is also crucial for fostering innovative thinking. Engaging in activities like playing a musical instrument, painting, writing, or cooking can broaden your perspective and enhance your creativity. These hobbies not only provide a mental break from work but also stimulate your brain in different ways, leading to new insights and ideas. Exposure to different fields and disciplines can lead to the cross-pollination of ideas. For example, learning about biology can inspire technological innovations, and studying architecture can influence design thinking in various contexts. **Collaboration and networking** play a significant role in fostering innovation. Collaborating with others can bring new insights and perspectives that you might not have considered on your own. Engage with people from different backgrounds and fields to exchange ideas and challenge your thinking. Networking events, conferences, and online communities offer excellent opportunities to meet like-minded individuals and gain inspiration from their experiences and ideas. By integrating these practices into your daily routine, you can continuously enhance your creative potential and drive meaningful innovation. Personal experiences often provide the most compelling evidence of how effective certain techniques can be in fostering innovation and creativity. Throughout my career and personal life, I have applied various methods to cultivate and enhance my creative thinking, and these anecdotes illustrate their success. One technique that has profoundly influenced my creativity is embracing curiosity and continuous learning. Early in my career, I developed a habit of reading widely on diverse topics. This practice not only expanded my knowledge base but also opened my mind to different perspectives. For instance, reading about psychology gave me insights into team dynamics, which improved collaboration and innovation in my projects. The cross-disciplinary knowledge I gained from these readings often led to breakthrough ideas that I could apply in my work. Challenging assumptions and embracing failure have also been crucial in my journey. There was a particularly challenging project where traditional methods were not yielding the desired results. By questioning our initial approach and considering unconventional methods, we eventually found a solution that not only worked but set a new standard in our field. Embracing failure has been equally important. Each setback provided valuable lessons and pushed me to think differently. For example, when a business venture didn't succeed, it forced me to pivot and explore new opportunities, ultimately leading to greater success. Regularly taking time to reflect helped me understand my creative processes better and identify areas for improvement. Creating a stimulating environment has been another effective strategy. My workspace is filled with books, art, and memorabilia that inspire me. Changing my environment by working from different locations, such as a quiet park or a bustling café, often sparked new ideas and perspectives. These practices consistently fueled my creativity and innovation. Engaging in creative exercises such as brainstorming and mind mapping has been instrumental in generating innovative ideas. Regular brainstorming sessions, both alone and with my team, produced a multitude of ideas, some of which led to successful projects. Mind mapping helped organize my thoughts and revealed connections that were not initially obvious. In conclusion, these personal anecdotes demonstrate the effectiveness of various ways of fostering innovation and creativity. By embracing curiosity, challenging assumptions, creating stimulating environments, and engaging in creative exercises, I have been able to cultivate a creative mindset and drive meaningful innovation in my work and personal life. Developing a creative mindset and fostering innovative thinking are crucial for navigating the complexities of the modern world.

Innovation is not a one-time event but a continuous process that requires sustained effort. Fostering an environment that maintains and enhances creativity over time is crucial for achieving consistent breakthroughs. In this section, we will explore how to sustain creativity, discuss the roles of environment, collaboration, and continuous learning, and provide examples of innovative breakthroughs resulting from these techniques. Maintaining and enhancing creativity over time requires deliberate and sustained efforts. Establishing routine creative practices is a foundational step. Regular engagement in creative exercises, such as brainstorming sessions and mind mapping, ensures a steady flow of ideas. Incorporating "creative sprints" into your schedule, where you focus intensely on generating ideas or solving problems for a set period, can sustain creative momentum. Encouraging risk-taking and experimentation is also crucial. Creating an environment that welcomes experimentation without fear of failure promotes a culture of creativity. Embracing a "fail fast, learn faster" approach allows failures to be seen as valuable learning opportunities, accelerating the innovation process. Diversifying your input is another effective strategy. Exposure to a variety of disciplines and perspectives fuels creativity. Engaging with different fields, attending conferences, and reading widely provide new insights that can be applied to your work. Collaborating with individuals from diverse backgrounds leads to the cross-pollination of ideas, fostering innovative thinking. Implementing feedback loops is essential for refining ideas and maintaining creativity. Establishing a system where ideas can be reviewed and iterated upon helps improve their quality and feasibility. Encouraging constructive criticism within a supportive environment ensures feedback is used positively to enhance creativity. By integrating these strategies, individuals and teams can create a sustainable environment for innovation, continually generating fresh ideas and solutions. These deliberate practices foster a culture of creativity that can adapt and thrive in a rapidly changing world. The environment plays a crucial role in fostering creativity and innovation. Remote work and digital nomadism show that changing scenery and experiencing different cultures can greatly enhance creativity. Leveraging digital tools further facilitates creativity, especially in distributed teams. Collaborative software and virtual brainstorming tools, like Miro, Trello, and Slack, enable seamless idea sharing and project management. Emerging technologies like virtual reality (VR) and augmented reality (AR) offer immersive experiences that enhance creative processes and collaboration. By creating a stimulating physical environment, adapting to various workspaces, and leveraging digital tools, individuals and teams can enhance their creative potential. A supportive and dynamic environment is essential for continuous innovation, allowing fresh ideas to flourish and evolve. Collaboration is vital for fostering innovation and creativity. A collaborative culture values teamwork over competition, encouraging the sharing of ideas and collective problem-solving. Regular team meetings and brainstorming sessions create opportunities for collaborative idea generation and innovation. Building diverse teams is crucial for generating richer and more innovative solutions. Teams composed of individuals from various backgrounds, disciplines, and skill sets bring different perspectives and experiences. This diversity leads to the cross-pollination of ideas, sparking creativity. Interdisciplinary collaboration, for instance, combining insights from technology, biology, and design, can result in groundbreaking innovations. Open communication is fundamental to effective collaboration. Transparent and inclusive communication channels, where everyone feels comfortable sharing their ideas, enhance creativity. Collaborative tools like shared documents, video conferencing, and instant messaging platforms ensure smooth communication and easy sharing of ideas. By fostering a collaborative culture, building diverse teams, and encouraging open communication, organizations can create an environment where creativity thrives. Collaboration not only enhances the quality and feasibility of ideas but also drives continuous innovation, leading to significant breakthroughs and advancements. Continuous learning is a cornerstone of sustained creativity and innovation. Committing to lifelong learning ensures that individuals remain adaptable and open to new ideas. Engaging in online courses, workshops, and reading keeps knowledge and skills up-to-date, fostering a mindset that is always ready to explore and innovate. Staying updated with industry trends is crucial for maintaining relevance and forward-thinking creativity. Subscribing to industry journals, attending webinars, and participating in professional networks helps individuals anticipate changes and innovate proactively. Understanding emerging technologies and market shifts allows for timely and informed innovation. Encouraging curiosity and exploration is essential for continuous learning. A curious mindset drives individuals to explore new areas and ask questions, leading to novel ideas and solutions. Creating opportunities for exploration, such as "innovation days" where employees can work on passion projects, can spark creativity and lead to unexpected breakthroughs. By committing to lifelong learning, staying updated with industry trends, and fostering curiosity, individuals and organizations can continuously enhance their creative potential. Continuous learning not only equips people with the skills needed to navigate a dynamic world but also sustains the innovative spirit necessary for long-term success. 3M's invention of Post-it Notes highlights the power of experimentation and collaboration. Spencer

Silver's accidental discovery of a weak adhesive, combined with Art Fry's creative application for bookmarking, resulted in one of 3M's most successful products. This example demonstrates the importance of a culture that supports unconventional ideas and collaborative efforts. IDEO's design thinking approach is another excellent illustration of innovation driven by collaboration and iterative processes. By emphasizing empathy, ideation, and prototyping, IDEO has developed numerous groundbreaking products and solutions across various industries. Their redesign of the shopping cart, for example, showcases how a human-centered, collaborative approach can lead to innovative breakthroughs. These examples illustrate that fostering a creative environment, encouraging experimentation, and leveraging collaboration are key to achieving innovative breakthroughs. Organizations that prioritize these elements can continuously generate fresh ideas and maintain a competitive edge in their respective fields. Fostering innovation requires deliberate strategies to maintain and enhance creativity over time. By establishing routine creative practices, encouraging risk-taking and experimentation, diversifying input, and implementing feedback loops, you can create a sustainable environment for innovation. The roles of environment, collaboration, and continuous learning are crucial in this process, providing the necessary support and stimulation for creative thinking. Examples like Google's "20% Time" policy, 3M's Post-it Notes, and IDEO's design thinking approach demonstrate the effectiveness of these techniques in driving innovative breakthroughs. By adopting these, you can cultivate a culture of innovation that continuously generates fresh ideas and solutions.

Innovation thrives when we adopt diverse approaches and deliberately practice methods to cultivate creative thinking. Embracing diverse learning and cross-disciplinary exploration is essential for fostering creativity and innovation. By engaging with a variety of subjects and experiences, individuals can develop a broad knowledge base that allows for unique connections and insights. This approach involves deliberately seeking out learning opportunities in fields unrelated to one's primary focus. For instance, studying psychology can provide valuable insights into team dynamics, while learning about design principles can enhance product development plans. This breadth of knowledge enables the synthesis of ideas from different domains, leading to innovative solutions. In my own career, I have consciously pursued diverse learning experiences. By exploring areas outside my immediate expertise, I have been able to apply new perspectives to my work, resulting in creative and effective outcomes. For example, understanding psychology has improved my leadership skills, while knowledge of design has influenced my approach to project management. To cultivate this habit, create a learning schedule that includes topics outside your main area of expertise. Allocate time each week for exploring new subjects through books, online courses, or discussions with experts. This practice enhances your ability to think creatively and innovate across various fields. Embracing a deep dive with intense focus is a powerful method for mastering new skills and fostering innovation. This approach involves dedicating focused periods to intensely study and practice a specific subject or skill. By immersing yourself fully, you can rapidly acquire expertise and apply it creatively in various contexts. In my own experience, deep dives have been transformative. For instance, when I aimed to improve my public speaking, I committed to an intense period of learning. I attended workshops, practiced regularly, and studied renowned speakers. This focused effort not only enhanced my skills quickly but also allowed me to incorporate new techniques in diverse situations, boosting my overall effectiveness. To implement this method, identify a skill or subject you wish to master. Create a structured plan with clear goals and deadlines, and dedicate uninterrupted time each day to your learning journey. For example, if you want to learn a new programming language, spend an hour daily practicing and studying, using online platforms and working on projects to apply your knowledge. This intense focus accelerates learning and fosters a deep understanding, enabling you to innovate and excel in your chosen area. By regularly embracing deep dives, you can continuously enhance your skills and drive meaningful progress. Experimentation and iterative learning are crucial for fostering innovation and continuous improvement. This method involves trying out new ideas, learning from failures, and making ongoing adjustments to refine solutions. Embracing a mindset of experimentation allows you to explore possibilities and discover what works best, leading to more effective and innovative outcomes. In my career, adopting an experimental approach has been invaluable. For example, while developing a new product, I created prototypes, tested them, gathered user feedback, and made iterative improvements. This cycle of experimentation and learning not only refined the product but also led to innovative features that better meet user needs. Each iteration provided insights that guided the next steps, ensuring continuous enhancement. To practice this method, start a project where you can apply iterative learning. Begin with a prototype or initial version, test it in real-world scenarios, collect feedback, and make necessary adjustments. This approach is applicable in various fields, such as writing, design, or product development. Embrace the learning process, view failures as valuable lessons, and continuously iterate based on feedback and new insights. By fostering a culture of experimentation and iterative learning, you can drive innovation, improve solutions, and achieve greater success in your endeavors. Meta-learning, or learning how to learn, is a vital skill for optimizing your ability to acquire new knowledge and skills efficiently. It involves understanding your personal learning processes and tailoring them to enhance creativity and productivity. By reflecting on past learning experiences and identifying effective procedures, you can continuously improve how you learn. In my own journey, meta-learning has been transformative. By analyzing which methods worked best for me, such as visual aids and hands-on practice, I tailored my approach to maximize learning outcomes. For instance, when studying complex concepts, I incorporated more diagrams and practical exercises, which significantly improved my comprehension and retention. To practice meta-learning, start by reflecting on your previous learning experiences. Identify the methods that were most effective and experiment with different learning methods, such as teaching others, using visual aids, or engaging in hands-on activities. Keep a learning journal to track your progress and refine your schemes based on what you discover. By mastering meta-learning, you can enhance your ability to learn efficiently and creatively. This skill not only accelerates personal growth but also equips you with the tools to adapt to new challenges and continuously innovate in your field. Time blocking and structured learning sessions are effective for fostering continuous learning and creativity. By allocating specific periods for focused learning and creative activities, you can enhance productivity and ensure consistent progress. In my experience, time blocking has been instrumental in maintaining a balanced and productive routine. By setting aside dedicated blocks of time each day for reading, brainstorming, and skill development, I've been able to make significant advancements in various areas. This structured approach ensures that I prioritize my learning goals and avoid distractions. To implement this method, create a weekly schedule with dedicated time blocks for different activities. For example, reserve an hour every morning for reading and another hour in the afternoon for creative projects or skill-building exercises. Stick to this schedule to establish a routine that prioritizes continuous learning and innovation. By consistently dedicating time to structured learning sessions, you can develop a disciplined approach to self-improvement. This not only enhances your ability to acquire new skills and knowledge but also fosters a mindset of continuous growth and creativity. Through time blocking, you can effectively manage your time and drive meaningful progress in your personal and professional endeavors. Leveraging technology and tools is essential for enhancing learning experiences and managing creative projects effectively. Digital tools streamline workflows, facilitate collaboration, and provide access to vast resources, driving productivity and innovation. In my work, integrating various digital tools has significantly improved my efficiency and creativity. Mind mapping software helps organize ideas, project management tools like Trello track progress, and online courses offer structured learning. These tools enable seamless idea development and project execution, allowing me to focus on creative problem-solving. To implement this strategy, explore and adopt digital tools that support your learning and creative processes. For example, use Evernote for note-taking, Coursera for online learning, and Slack for team communication. Experiment with different tools to find the ones that best fit your needs and enhance your productivity. By effectively leveraging technology, you can optimize your workflows and enhance your ability to innovate. These tools not only improve organization and efficiency but also provide platforms for continuous learning and collaboration. Embracing digital solutions ensures that you stay ahead in a rapidly evolving world, driving meaningful progress and creative breakthroughs in your personal and professional endeavors. Collaboration and knowledge sharing are vital for fostering innovation and enhancing learning experiences. By working together and exchanging ideas, individuals can leverage collective creativity and develop more effective solutions. In my career, collaboration has been key to my creative development.

Engaging with colleagues, participating in mastermind groups, and attending industry conferences have provided valuable insights and feedback. These collaborative efforts have shaped my innovative projects and driven significant progress. To implement this strategy, join or create a mastermind group with peers who share similar interests. Regularly meet to discuss ideas, share knowledge, and provide feedback on each other's projects. Participate in online forums and attend conferences to expand your network and gain diverse perspectives that can inspire your creativity. By fostering a collaborative environment, you encourage open communication and the sharing of diverse viewpoints, which are crucial for innovation. Knowledge sharing not only enhances individual learning but also builds a supportive community that drives continuous improvement. Embracing collaboration and knowledge sharing ensures that you harness the collective intelligence and creativity of your network, leading to greater success in your personal and professional endeavors. By adopting these unique methods, you can develop innovative strategies to enhance your creativity and problem-solving abilities. Embrace diverse learning, deep dive with intense focus, experiment iteratively, optimize your learning processes, use time blocking, leverage technology, and foster collaboration. These plans, supported by practical exercises, can help you cultivate a creative mindset and drive meaningful innovation in your personal and professional life.

Implementing the "Warrior Mindset 2.0" in Daily Life

In this chapter, we'll explore how to integrate the principles of the "Warrior Mindset 2.0" into various aspects of your daily life. We'll cover practical applications at work, in relationships, and in your personal growth journey. By the end of this chapter, you'll have actionable strategies and exercises to help you embody the techniques discussed throughout this book. Applying the principles of the book isn't just about theoretical understanding; it's about real-world execution. The concepts we've discussed so far are powerful, but their true strength lies in their application. It's one thing to understand this field in an abstract sense, but it's another to live it every day, especially when faced with modern challenges like economic uncertainty, rapid technological changes, and the constant bombardment of information. We will delve into how you can enhance your professional life by incorporating tenacity and decision-making efficiency into your work routine. Whether you're aiming for a promotion, managing a team, or navigating a career transition, this know-how will provide you with a competitive edge and a robust mindset to handle workplace pressures. Next, we'll look at how the fighter mindset can strengthen your relationships. Personal and professional relationships require a delicate balance of empathy and communication. I'll share insights and anecdotes that demonstrate how applying these principles can lead to more meaningful and supportive connections. Finally, we'll focus on personal growth. It isn't just about external achievements; it's about internal development. You'll learn how to set and achieve personal goals, overcome setbacks, and maintain a growth-oriented mindset. This section will provide you with practical tools to continuously improve and adapt, turning adversity into opportunity. Throughout this chapter, I'll share exercises and action plans that I've developed and used, including those that my brother and I have practiced together. These exercises are designed to help you build adaptability, enhance your performance, and maintain a positive, forward-thinking attitude. The journey to integrating the "Warrior Mindset 2.0" into your daily life is not a quick fix but a continuous process of growth and adaptation. It's about making small, consistent changes that lead to significant improvements over time. As you read on, I encourage you to actively participate in the exercises and reflect on how you can incorporate them into your unique context. By the end of this chapter, you will have a comprehensive toolkit to help you implement the mindset in all areas of your life. Remember, the goal is not perfection but progress. Every step you take towards applying these principles will bring you closer to becoming the resilient, high-performing individual you aspire to be. Let's dive in and start transforming these powerful concepts into practical actions that will enhance your work, relationships, and personal growth.

Enhancing performance at work is crucial in today's high-stress professional environment. The principles of the book can provide the edge you need to excel and thrive. Developing mental fortitude is a key strategy; it involves maintaining focus, staying calm under pressure, and bouncing back from setbacks. Techniques such as visualization, positive self-talk, and setting incremental goals can fortify your mental stability. Dynamic resilience is another crucial aspect. It means being adaptable to change and open to new approaches. This can be achieved by continuously learning, seeking feedback, and maintaining curiosity about new developments in your field. Embracing change as an opportunity rather than a threat fosters a growth mindset, enabling you to thrive amidst uncertainty. Efficient decision-making is vital in high-pressure environments. Rapid, effective decision-making can be streamlined by setting clear priorities and using decision-making frameworks. This approach ensures that you can quickly weigh options, trust your instincts, and learn from past decisions, leading to better outcomes under pressure. Maintaining focus and attention is increasingly challenging in the era of digital distractions. Strategies such as time-blocking, minimizing multitasking, and creating a conducive work environment can help sustain focus. Incorporating mindfulness practices and regular breaks also enhances attention span and productivity. These approaches provide a robust foundation for handling workplace stress, adapting to change, making swift decisions, and maintaining high productivity levels, ensuring sustained professional growth and success. These principles have been successfully applied in various professional scenarios, illustrating their effectiveness.

During a high-stakes project, our team faced numerous obstacles, including tight deadlines and limited resources. By applying endurance, like breaking the project into manageable tasks and using positive self-talk, we maintained focus and motivation. Visualization techniques helped us stay centered on the end goal, reducing anxiety and preserving team morale. This approach allowed us to meet our objectives despite significant challenges.

One of my coaching clients transitioned to a new role in a different industry, initially feeling overwhelmed. Viewing the transition as a growth opportunity, they embraced change, adapted to new challenges, and ultimately excelled in their new role. This experience underscores the importance of adaptability and a growth mindset in navigating professional changes.

During organizational restructuring, I had to make several rapid decisions impacting my team's future. Utilizing a decision-making framework that prioritized key factors and balanced data with intuition, I made informed decisions quickly. This approach mitigated risks and provided clear direction, helping the team navigate a tumultuous period. The ability to make swift, effective decisions is crucial in high-pressure environments.

These are some exercises that could help you in your day-to-day life:

Exercise 1: Daily Mental Toughness Routine

Morning Visualization: Spend 5-10 minutes each morning visualizing your day. Picture yourself handling challenges calmly and effectively, achieving your goals, and maintaining a positive attitude.

Positive Self-Talk: Create a list of positive affirmations related to your work. Repeat these affirmations daily, especially during stressful moments.

Incremental Goals: Break your larger work goals into smaller, achievable tasks. Focus on completing these tasks one at a time, celebrating small victories along the way.

Exercise 2: Building Dynamic Resilience

Continuous Learning: Dedicate at least 30 minutes each day to learning something new related to your field. This could be through reading articles, taking online courses, or attending webinars.

Feedback Loop: Regularly seek feedback from colleagues and supervisors. Use this feedback constructively to improve your performance and adaptability.

Embrace Change: Identify one change in your work environment each week and find ways to adapt to it positively. This could involve adopting a new tool, trying a different workflow, or adjusting to new team dynamics.

Exercise 3: Enhancing Focus and Attention

Time-Blocking: Allocate specific blocks of time for different tasks throughout your day. During these blocks, focus solely on the task at hand, avoiding all distractions.

Mindfulness Practice: Incorporate short awareness exercises into your daily routine. This could be as simple as a 5-minute breathing exercise or a brief meditation session.

Breaks and Downtime: Schedule regular breaks throughout your workday to recharge. Use these breaks to step away from your workspace, stretch, or take a short walk.

To effectively implement the "Warrior Mindset 2.0" at work, start with a comprehensive assessment of your current work habits, identifying areas where performance need improvement. This initial step sets the foundation for targeted growth and development. Next, set specific, measurable goals for enhancing these areas. For instance, if you struggle with staying focused, your goal might be to practice time-blocking techniques daily. Clear goals provide direction and motivation, ensuring you stay on track. Develop a daily and weekly routine that incorporates the principles of perseverance, efficient decision-making, and sustained focus. Consistency is key, start each day with a morning visualization exercise to mentally prepare for the challenges ahead. Incorporate positive self-talk throughout the day to maintain a resilient mindset. To track your progress, keep a journal or log. Document your daily achievements, setbacks, and reflections. This practice helps you identify patterns, adjust strategies, and stay accountable to your goals. Regularly reviewing your progress ensures continuous improvement and adaptability. Engage with a supportive community. Share your journey, engaging with a community provides valuable support, motivation, and new insights. It also fosters a sense of accountability and belonging, enhancing your commitment to the it. Finally, prioritize self-care.

Applying the this to personal and professional relationships can significantly improve the quality and depth of your interactions. Relationships are fundamental to our well-being and success, and the principles of the "Warrior Mindset 2.0" can help you build stronger, more resilient connections. This section explores how to apply these principles, shares anecdotes to illustrate their positive impact, and provides exercises and action plans for enhancing your relationships. Central to this approach is empathy, which involves understanding and sharing the feelings of others. By actively listening and showing genuine interest in others' perspectives, you build trust and rapport, fostering a supportive environment. Effective communication is another key component. This attitude encourages clear, honest, and respectful dialogue, even when discussing difficult topics. This helps prevent misunderstandings and resolves conflicts more efficiently, ensuring that both your needs and the needs of others are met. Stability in relationships is equally important. Navigating conflicts and setbacks with grace and strength, and viewing challenges as opportunities for growth, helps maintain and strengthen bonds during difficult times. This teaches you to handle these situations with a positive, growth-oriented outlook. Finally, mutual support and encouragement are vital. By uplifting and encouraging those around you, you not only strengthen your relationships but also create a positive and empowering environment. Celebrating each other's successes and providing support during tough times fosters a sense of unity and cooperation. In summary, the principles of empathy, effective communication and mutual support can profoundly improve your relationships. By consistently practicing these principles, you build stronger, more resilient connections that enhance both your personal and professional life. In my previous role as a project manager, we faced a critical deadline that required intense collaboration and mutual support. When teaching, I emphasized empathy and understanding within the team. We held regular check-ins where everyone could voice their concerns and ideas. This open communication-built trust and allowed us to support each other effectively. When one team member struggled, others stepped in to help, knowing their support would be reciprocated. This approach not only helped us meet our deadline but also strengthened our team bond, making us more resilient for future challenges. Another good example is when a close friend and I had a significant disagreement that threatened our long-standing relationship. Instead of avoiding the conflict, I applied my own lessons by addressing the issue directly and empathetically. We sat down and had an honest conversation, where I listened to their perspective without interrupting and shared my feelings openly but respectfully. This approach helped us understand each other's viewpoints better and resolve the conflict amicably. The experience strengthened our relationship, teaching us the value of open and honest communication. Finally, a colleague was going through a tough time personally, which affected their performance at work. I reached out to offer support. We had several conversations where I simply listened, providing a safe space for them to express their concerns. I also shared some techniques that had helped me in the past. This support not only helped my colleague navigate their personal challenges but also strengthened our professional relationship, fostering a more supportive and collaborative work environment. These are some exercises that could help you in your day-to-day life:

Exercise 1: Active Listening Practice

Set Intentions: Before engaging in a conversation, set an intention to listen actively. This means focusing entirely on the speaker without planning your response.

Show Engagement: Use non-verbal cues such as nodding and maintaining eye contact to show that you are engaged.

Reflect and Clarify: Reflect back what the speaker has said to ensure understanding and ask clarifying questions if needed.

Practice Regularly: Incorporate active listening into your daily interactions to build stronger connections.

Exercise 2: Empathy Building Routine

Daily Reflection: At the end of each day, reflect on your interactions and identify moments where you could have shown more empathy.

Empathy Journaling: Write about these moments, exploring how you might approach them differently in the future.

Perspective-Taking: Regularly practice putting yourself in others' shoes, especially during conflicts or disagreements.

Apply in Real-Time: Use these insights to approach future interactions with greater empathy and understanding.

Exercise 3: Effective Communication Techniques

Assertive Expression: Practice expressing your needs and feelings assertively without being aggressive. Use "I" statements to communicate how you feel and what you need.

Constructive Feedback: When giving feedback, focus on specific behaviors rather than personal attributes. Use a positive, constructive tone.

Conflict Resolution: During conflicts, aim to understand the other person's perspective fully before responding. Seek win-win solutions that address both parties' needs.

Regular Check-Ins: Establish regular check-ins with key relationships, both personal and professional, to discuss any issues and celebrate successes.

To strengthen your relationships using the "Warrior Mindset 2.0," start with a thorough assessment of your current interactions, identifying areas for improvement in empathy, communication and support. Set specific, measurable goals for each relationship, such as scheduling weekly check-ins with a close friend or providing more regular feedback to colleagues. Develop consistent routines, for example, practice daily reflection on your interactions to identify opportunities for showing more empathy and apply these insights in future conversations. Track your progress by keeping a journal, reflecting on what worked well and what could be improved, and making necessary adjustments. Engage with supportive communities or seek out relationship-building workshops to gain new insights and motivation from others. Regularly celebrate your successes to reinforce positive behaviors and encourage continued growth. By following this action plan, you can enhance both your personal and professional relationships, fostering a more connected and supportive environment. By applying these principles to your relationships, you can build stronger, more resilient connections. Through consistent practice and a commitment to growth, you can enhance both your personal and professional relationships, leading to a more connected and supportive life.

Personal growth is a continuous journey of self-improvement and adaptation. This section will explore ways of using being a champion to foster personal growth, share personal stories of growth and transformation, and provide exercises and action plans to help you on your journey. This book provides powerful techniques for personal growth. Firstly, setting clear, achievable goals is essential. Define your objectives and break them down into manageable tasks to track your progress and stay motivated. Embracing challenges is another key principle; view obstacles as opportunities for growth, stepping out of your comfort zone to tackle difficulties head-on. This mindset transforms setbacks into valuable learning experiences. Developing resilience is crucial. Commit to continuous learning. Expand your knowledge and skills through formal education, reading, and new experiences, staying curious and open to new ideas. Finally, regular self-reflection is vital for understanding your strengths and weaknesses. Analyze your actions and decisions to identify areas for improvement and make necessary adjustments. Journaling is an effective tool for this practice.

A few years ago, I found myself feeling stagnant in my career. Despite working hard, I wasn't achieving the growth I desired. Applying the fighter mindset, I set clear goals for my career progression and embraced the challenges ahead. I sought out new learning opportunities, attended workshops, and connected with mentors. Through continuous learning, I overcame obstacles and achieved significant career advancement. This transformation taught me the power of setting clear goals and embracing challenges. After my brother's accident, I struggled emotionally. These methods helped me develop the strength and balance needed to navigate this difficult period. I practiced mindfulness and meditation daily, which helped me stay grounded and focused. Positive self-talk reinforced my stamina, allowing me to support my brother and continue my personal growth journey. Another pivotal moment in my personal growth journey was committing to lifelong learning. Realizing that complacency was hindering my development, I made a conscious effort to seek out new knowledge and skills. I enrolled in courses, read extensively, and engaged in diverse experiences. This commitment to continuous learning opened up new opportunities and perspectives, fueling my personal and professional growth. Here's a bunch of more exercises!

Exercise 1: Goal Setting and Planning

Identify Goals: Write down your short-term and long-term goals. Ensure they are specific, measurable, achievable, relevant, and time-bound (SMART).

Break Down Goals: Divide your goals into smaller, manageable tasks. Create a timeline for achieving these tasks.

Track Progress: Regularly review your progress and adjust your plan as needed. Celebrate small victories to stay motivated.

Exercise 2: Embracing Challenges

Step Out of Your Comfort Zone: Identify areas in your life where you tend to stay within your comfort zone. Set a goal to take one small step outside this zone each week.

Reflect on Challenges: After facing a challenge, reflect on what you learned and how you grew from the experience. Write about it in a journal.

Seek New Experiences: Actively seek out new experiences that challenge you. This could be learning a new skill, taking on a new project, or exploring a new hobby.

Exercise 3: Continuous Learning

Daily Learning: Dedicate at least 30 minutes each day to learning something new. This could be reading, taking an online course, or exploring a new topic.

Expand Horizons: Engage in activities that expose you to new ideas and perspectives. Attend workshops, join discussion groups, or travel.

Reflect and Apply: Reflect on what you learn and think about how you can apply this knowledge to your personal and professional life.

To foster personal growth with this state of mind, start with a thorough self-assessment to identify your strengths and areas needing improvement. Set specific, measurable, achievable, relevant, and time-bound (SMART) goals for both short-term and long-term growth. Develop a consistent daily and weekly routine that includes mindfulness exercises, positive self-talk, and dedicated learning time. Track your progress by keeping a journal. Reflect on your achievements, setbacks, and insights, making adjustments to your plan as needed. Engaging with supportive communities or joining personal growth groups can provide motivation and new perspectives, enhancing your journey. Celebrate your successes regularly, no matter how small, to reinforce positive behaviors and maintain motivation. By following this action plan—assessing your current state, setting clear goals, developing consistent routines, tracking progress, engaging with communities, and celebrating successes—you can effectively use these lessons to achieve significant personal growth. Stay committed, be patient with yourself, and recognize every step forward as a victory in your continuous journey of self-improvement.

Stay committed, be patient with yourself, and celebrate every step forward.

In this chapter, we explored how the "Warrior Mindset 2.0" can significantly enhance your personal and professional relationships and foster substantial personal growth. We discussed applying it to relationships through empathy, effective communication and mutual support. Personal anecdotes illustrated the positive impact of these principles, showcasing real-life examples of strengthened bonds and improved connections. We then delved into methods for achieving personal growth; setting clear, achievable goals, embracing challenges, committing to continuous learning and practicing self-reflection are all essential steps in this journey. These means, grounded in the principles we sprinkled throughout the book, provide a solid foundation for ongoing self-improvement. Finally, we outlined a comprehensive action plan for personal growth. This plan involves assessing your current state, setting SMART goals, developing consistent routines, tracking progress, engaging with supportive communities, and celebrating your successes. The principles discussed in this chapter are not merely theoretical; they are practical tools designed to transform your life. Start by implementing small changes today. Remember, personal growth is a journey, not a destination. Each step you take brings you closer to becoming the resilient, high-performing individual you aspire to be. Embrace the challenges that come your way and view them as opportunities for growth. When you face setbacks, remember that this is about bouncing back stronger. Keep pushing forward, and don't be afraid to step out of your comfort zone. The greatest growth often comes from the most challenging experiences. Stay committed to continuous learning. Seek out new knowledge and experiences that broaden your horizons and enhance your skills. Engage with others who share your goals and aspirations, and learn from their experiences. Surround yourself with a supportive community that encourages your growth and provides valuable insights. Celebrate your successes, no matter how small. Recognizing and celebrating your achievements reinforces positive behavior and keeps you motivated. Every step forward is a victory, and each milestone you reach is a testament to your strength and determination. The book offers a powerful framework for enhancing your relationships and achieving personal growth. By applying these principles and following the action plan, you can transform your life! Start today. Embrace these lessons and embark on your journey toward becoming the best version of yourself. The path may be challenging, but the rewards are immense. Your journey of self-improvement and growth begins now. Take the first step, and keep moving forward with courage, determination, and resilience.

Conclusion

As we've journeyed through the realms of resilience and performance, we've redefined what it means to possess a Warrior Mindset. We've tackled contemporary challenges, learned new strategies, and embraced the science behind mental fortitude. It isn't just about surviving; it's about thriving in an ever-changing world. It's about turning obstacles into opportunities and setbacks into setups for an even greater comeback. In this final chapter, we look forward to the future. We'll explore how our mindset can and must continue to evolve to meet new challenges head-on. Whether it's the rapid pace of technological change, global crises, or personal setbacks, the future demands a mindset that's not just strong but also flexible and adaptable. Prepare to adapt, grow, and conquer whatever comes your way. Together, we'll ensure that this is not just a philosophy but a living, breathing, ever-evolving force within you. Let's dive into how you can be ready for tomorrow's challenges today, using every experience as a stepping stone towards greater strength.

As we peer into the future, it's clear that the challenges we face will be both diverse and complex. Technological advancements such as artificial intelligence and automation promise to revolutionize industries but also bring uncertainties regarding job security and skill requirements. Digital overload and cybersecurity threats will demand a resilient approach to maintaining inner clarity and protecting personal information. Global crises, including climate change, pandemics, and political instability, will continue to test our adaptability. These crises necessitate a mindset that is not only strong but also flexible, capable of rapid response and recovery. On a personal level, future setbacks will include career and financial challenges, mental health issues, and evolving social dynamics. The need for continuous learning, emotional intelligence, and adaptable fitness routines will be paramount. The lessons must evolve to meet these challenges head-on. Embracing lifelong learning, enhancing digital elasticity and cultivating a growth mindset will be essential. By viewing challenges as opportunities and learning from failures, we can transform obstacles into stepping stones for growth. The future will demand a mindset that is ever-evolving, ready to adapt and thrive in the face of adversity. The future will undoubtedly present a series of global crises that will test our patience and adaptability. Climate change remains a significant threat, bringing about more frequent and severe natural disasters, resource scarcity, and environmental degradation. These changes will require not only physical adaptability but also strength of mind to cope with the stress and uncertainty they bring. Health crises, such as pandemics, are another inevitable challenge. The COVID-19 pandemic has taught us the importance of rapid response and flexibility in the face of global health threats. Future pandemics will demand a resilient mindset, capable of handling prolonged periods of uncertainty and change. Political and economic instability will also pose significant challenges. Shifts in political landscapes and economic turbulence can lead to periods of stress and anxiety, impacting our emotional well-being. It will be essential to develop a Warrior Mindset that is both robust and flexible, allowing us to navigate these turbulent times with confidence. To face these global crises, we must enhance our emotional intelligence, cultivate a growth mindset, and build strong support networks. By viewing these challenges as opportunities for growth, we can transform adversity into a catalyst for personal and collective development, ensuring that we emerge stronger and more resilient. In the journey of life, personal setbacks are inevitable. Career and financial challenges are common, especially in a rapidly changing job market where adaptability is crucial. Job losses, career changes, and financial instability require a resilient mindset that embraces continuous learning and innovation. Mental health issues, such as stress, anxiety, and depression, are increasingly prevalent in today's world. Navigating these challenges demands emotional intelligence, self-awareness, and robust coping mechanisms. Developing mindfulness practices and seeking professional help when needed can fortify our minds. Social dynamics are also evolving, presenting unique personal challenges. The pressures of maintaining an online presence, managing relationships, and dealing with societal expectations can be overwhelming. Building strong interpersonal skills and a supportive network is essential for navigating these complexities. To overcome personal setbacks, we must cultivate a growth mindset that views challenges as opportunities for growth. Embracing failures as learning experiences and maintaining flexibility in our approach to life's obstacles will transform adversity into a powerful catalyst for personal development. By adopting these principles, we can turn setbacks into setups for even greater comebacks, emerging stronger and more resilient in the face of life's inevitable challenges. In an era where job roles and required skills are constantly evolving, committing to lifelong learning is paramount. This means regularly updating our knowledge and skills through formal education, online courses, and self-study. Staying curious and open to new ideas fosters mental flexibility, allowing us to pivot and adapt when faced with unexpected challenges. The digital age brings benefits but also challenges like information overload and cybersecurity threats. To maintain inner clarity, we must incorporate regular digital detoxes, setting boundaries for screen time, and prioritizing offline activities. Additionally, staying informed about cybersecurity best practices—such as using strong passwords and two-factor authentication—helps protect our digital footprint. Strengthening Emotional Intelligence: Developing a deep understanding of our emotions and triggers is crucial for navigating stress. Enhancing empathy and communication skills improves interpersonal relationships, creating a supportive network. By fostering emotional intelligence, we can better manage our reactions and maintain stability during turbulent times.

Building Physical Resilience: Physical health is intrinsically linked to brain resilience. Implementing adaptable fitness routines ensures we stay fit regardless of circumstances, while mind-body practices like yoga and meditation strengthen the connection between our physical and psychical well-being.

Cultivating a Growth Mindset: Viewing challenges as opportunities for growth is a cornerstone of the Warrior Mindset 2.0. Embracing failures as learning experiences helps us analyze what went wrong and apply those lessons to future endeavors. This perspective shift transforms obstacles into stepping stones for personal development.

To fully grasp the adaptability and strength of this mindset, let's delve into some future scenarios and practical applications that illustrate its power.

Scenario 1: Rapid Job Market Changes Imagine your industry undergoes significant shifts due to automation. Jobs that once seemed secure are now redundant. You will be able to stay ahead by continuously learning and updating your skills. Engage in online courses, attend industry workshops, and network with professionals in emerging fields. By staying proactive, you remain competitive and adaptable, turning potential job loss into an opportunity for career growth and reinvention.

Scenario 2: Facing a Global Health Crisis Suppose another global health crisis emerges. Applying the champion mindset, you maintain rational flexibility and emotional intelligence. Develop a routine that includes physical exercise, digital detoxes, and mindfulness practices to manage stress. Stay informed through reliable sources, and build a supportive community around you. This approach not only helps you cope but also thrive, using the crisis as a platform to strengthen your adaptability.

Scenario 3: Navigating Personal Financial Challenges Financial instability can strike unexpectedly. You will be able to adapt by implementing budgeting techniques and seeking alternative income sources. Maintain rational flexibility through meditation and self-reflection. Use adversity as a catalyst to explore new opportunities and innovations, perhaps even turning a financial setback into a successful entrepreneurial venture.

Scenario 4: Managing Information Overload In an era of constant digital connectivity, maintaining focus can be challenging. Utilize digital detox strategies and set specific times for checking news and social media. Prioritize tasks using productivity tools like time-blocking and to-do lists. These practices help you maintain inner clarity, enhance decision-making, and increase overall productivity.

As we look to the future, it's essential to understand that the Warrior Mindset 2.0 is not a static set of principles but a dynamic, evolving approach to life. By anticipating future challenges and adapting our mindset accordingly, we can navigate the complexities of tomorrow with confidence. Remember, every challenge is an opportunity for growth, and every setback is a setup for a stronger comeback. Stay adaptable, stay resilient, and continue to evolve. The future is yours to conquer. Adaptability allows us to adjust to new conditions, which is crucial in a landscape where technological advancements, economic shifts, and global crises are common. Without adaptability, we risk becoming stagnant and unable to cope with evolving realities. Continuous learning ensures we remain relevant and competitive. As industries transform due to automation and artificial intelligence, the skills we possess today may become obsolete tomorrow. Embracing lifelong learning, through formal education, online courses, and self-study, keeps our knowledge and abilities sharp. It fosters a mindset open to new ideas and perspectives, which is vital for personal and professional growth. Personal setbacks, such as job loss or health crises, further underscore the need for adaptability and continuous learning. These challenges demand a resilient mindset that can navigate and overcome obstacles. By committing to constant self-improvement and remaining flexible in our approaches, we can turn adversity into opportunities for growth. In essence, the Warrior Mindset 2.0 thrives on the principles of adaptability and continuous learning, empowering us to face the uncertainties of the future with confidence. These traits are the bedrock of personal and professional success in an ever-changing world. Cultivating a growth mindset is essential for personal and professional development. This mindset, characterized by the belief that abilities and intelligence can be developed through dedication and hard work, enables us to embrace challenges and persist in the face of setbacks. Here are some effective strategies for maintaining a growth mindset:

Embrace Challenges: View challenges as opportunities for growth rather than obstacles. When faced with a difficult task, focus on what you can learn from the experience. This shift in perspective transforms how you approach problems, making you more resilient and innovative.

Learn from Criticism: Constructive criticism is a valuable tool for growth. Instead of taking feedback personally, use it to identify areas for improvement. This approach fosters a mindset that is open to learning and self-improvement. By viewing criticism as a means to grow rather than a setback, you build a foundation for continuous development.

Cultivate Curiosity: Stay curious about the world around you. Seek out new experiences, ask questions, and explore topics outside your comfort zone. Curiosity drives continuous learning and keeps your mind flexible and adaptable. This trait ensures that you are always on the lookout for new knowledge and skills.

Set Learning Goals: Establish specific, achievable learning goals. Whether it's mastering a new skill, reading a certain number of books, or completing an online course, setting goals keeps you motivated and focused on your growth journey. Clear objectives provide direction and purpose, making the process of learning more structured and rewarding.

Reflect Regularly: Take time to reflect on your experiences and what you've learned. Regular reflection helps you identify patterns, understand your strengths and weaknesses, and chart a course for future growth. This practice encourages a deeper understanding of your progress and areas that need improvement.

Surround Yourself with Growth-Minded Individuals: The people you interact with can significantly influence your mindset. Surround yourself with individuals who encourage learning and growth. Their positive influence can inspire you to adopt and maintain a growth mindset, creating a supportive environment that nurtures continuous improvement.

Practice Resilience: Cultivate it by facing difficulties head-on, maintaining a positive outlook, and developing coping strategies. Resilience strengthens your ability to adapt and grow from challenging situations, turning obstacles into opportunities for advancement.

By implementing them, you can maintain a growth mindset that empowers you to navigate challenges, embrace learning opportunities, and achieve continuous personal and professional growth. This mindset not only enhances your ability to succeed but also enriches your overall life experience.

Early in my career, I faced a significant challenge when the company I worked for underwent a major restructuring. Many of my colleagues were laid off, and those of us who remained were tasked with taking on additional responsibilities. Instead of viewing this as a burden, I saw it as an opportunity to learn new skills and demonstrate my value. This mindset shifts not only helped me survive the restructuring but also propelled my career forward as I gained new expertise and confidence. I remember a time when I received harsh feedback on a project, I was passionate about. Initially, I felt defensive and discouraged. However, I decided to look at the criticism objectively. I analyzed the feedback, identified areas for improvement, and sought advice from colleagues. This experience taught me the importance of accepting criticism as a tool for growth. By addressing the feedback constructively, I was able to refine my work and achieve better results. Throughout my life, I've made it a point to explore interests outside my professional field. Whether it's learning a new language, studying a different culture, or picking up a musical instrument, these pursuits have kept my mind flexible and open to new ideas. This curiosity has not only enriched my personal life but also enhanced my professional creativity and problem-solving abilities. After my brother's accident, I set a goal to learn more about neuroscience and psychology to better understand resilience and recovery. I enrolled in online courses, attended workshops, and read extensively on the subject. This goal-driven approach helped me gain valuable insights that I applied to my brother's rehabilitation and my own personal development.

Personal adversity is pivotal in shaping ourselves as we want to be. Challenges test our limits, compelling us to adapt and discover strengths we never knew we had. Through facing and overcoming difficulties, we build hardiness, enhancing our ability to recover quickly from setbacks and improving our overall performance. Adversity pushes us out of our comfort zones, forcing us to adapt to new circumstances where growth truly happens.

When encountering difficulties, we face a choice: succumb to pressure or rise to the occasion. Choosing the latter means developing problem-solving skills, emotional intelligence, and a stronger sense of self-efficacy. Each challenge we overcome adds to our strength, making us better equipped for future obstacles. Reframing adversity as a learning opportunity rather than a setback shifts our perspective, allowing us to ask, "What can I learn from this experience?" This mindset transforms how we approach and deal with challenges. Setting small, achievable goals provides a sense of accomplishment and momentum, making larger problems seem less daunting. Building a support network offers crucial advice, encouragement, and perspective, while self-care practices like exercise and mindfulness help maintain focus. Learning from failure is also essential, turning setbacks into stepping stones for future success. Notable examples of individuals who have turned adversity into growth include J.K. Rowling, Nelson Mandela, and Oprah Winfrey. J.K. Rowling faced numerous rejections and personal struggles before her perseverance led to the success of the Harry Potter series. Nelson Mandela used his 27 years in prison to reflect and plan for a future free of racial segregation, ultimately becoming South Africa's first black president. Oprah Winfrey overcame a tumultuous childhood to become a media mogul, using her experiences as a source of strength and empathy. Adversity, while challenging, is a powerful catalyst for growth. It develops elasticity, hones problem-solving skills, and strengthens emotional fortitude. With the right mindset, obstacles become opportunities for personal and professional development.

In facing adversity, we find the truest test of our mental balance and performance. This chapter has underscored the transformative power of personal challenges, illustrating how adversity pushes us to develop new strengths and uncover hidden potentials. By reframing difficulties as opportunities for growth, setting manageable goals, building supportive networks, practicing self-care, and learning from failures, we can turn setbacks into powerful catalysts for development. The stories of J.K. Rowling, Nelson Mandela, and Oprah Winfrey vividly demonstrate that the right mindset can transform even the most daunting obstacles into stepping stones for success. Their journeys highlight the importance of perseverance, adaptability, and an unwavering belief in one's ability to overcome challenges. As you navigate your own path, remember that each difficulty you face is an opportunity to build and enhance your performance. Now is the time to actively apply these principles in your life. Embrace challenges, seek out learning opportunities, and remain open to growth in all its forms. Your journey will be marked by ups and downs, but with a resilient mindset, you can turn every setback into a setup for a stronger comeback. As you move forward, let the lessons from this chapter inspire you to continuously develop and evolve. Your ability to grow through adversity will not only enhance your personal and professional life but also inspire those around you. The future is full of challenges, but it also holds limitless opportunities for those with the courage to seize them. Embrace your journey, trust in your strength, and keep pushing forward. Your greatest achievements lie ahead.

As you continue to develop your Warrior Mindset 2.0, leveraging additional resources can further enhance your psychological abilities. This chapter provides recommendations for further reading, tools, and resources to support your ongoing growth, as well as links to communities and support networks that can offer guidance and inspiration.

Motivational Thought

Believe in your inner strength, for every challenge is an opportunity to grow. With unwavering determination and resilience, you can overcome any obstacle, transforming adversity into fuel for success. Remember: the greatest victories often come from the most difficult battles, and with the Warrior Mindset, there is nothing you cannot achieve.

Further Readings

"Peak Performance" by Brad Stulberg and Steve Magness This book delves into the science of high performance, offering practical advice on how to achieve your best without sacrificing health and happiness. It's a must-read for anyone looking to push their limits while maintaining balance.

"Range: Why Generalists Triumph in a Specialized World" by David Epstein Epstein's exploration of how a broad range of experiences can lead to greater success is essential for those looking to diversify their skills and approaches. It reinforces the importance of adaptability and lifelong learning.

"The Art of Impossible" by Steven Kotler Kotler's insights into the science of achieving the extraordinary provide a roadmap for pushing boundaries and maximizing potential. His emphasis on motivation, learning, and creativity aligns perfectly with the Warrior Mindset 2.0.

"Atomic Habits" by James Clear Clear's guide to building good habits and breaking bad ones is invaluable for anyone looking to implement lasting change. His practical schemes can help you maintain resilience and focus in the face of adversity.

"Ultralearning" by Scott H. Young This book offers strategies for mastering hard skills quickly and efficiently. Young's methods for aggressive self-directed learning are perfect for those committed to continuous improvement.

"Burnout: The Secret to Unlocking the Stress Cycle" by Emily Nagoski and Amelia Nagoski Understanding how to manage stress and prevent burnout is crucial for maintaining long-term resilience.

The Nagoski sisters provide actionable advice for handling stress effectively.

Tools and Resources

1. **Mindfulness and Meditation Apps**
   - **Headspace**: Offers guided meditations and mindfulness exercises to help reduce stress and improve focus.
   - **Calm**: Provides a variety of meditation practices, sleep aids, and relaxation techniques to support mental well-being.

2. **Productivity Tools**
   - **Trello**: A versatile project management tool that helps organize tasks and goals effectively.
   - **Evernote**: A note-taking app that can help you keep track of ideas, plans, and reflections.

3. **Learning Platforms**
   - **Coursera**: Offers online courses from top universities on a wide range of subjects, allowing you to continuously expand your knowledge.
   - **Udemy**: Provides a vast array of courses on professional and personal development topics.

4. **Fitness and Wellness Apps**
   - **MyFitnessPal**: A comprehensive app for tracking diet and exercise, helping you maintain physical resilience.
   - **Strava**: A social network

Appendix

Resilience and Performance Exercises

Mental Toughness Drills

Exercise 1: Cold Exposure

Objective: Build mental toughness and resilience.

Description: Take cold showers or ice baths for a specific duration.

Duration: Start with 30 seconds and gradually increase to 5 minutes.

Instructions: Focus on controlling your breath and maintaining calm. Reflect on your mental state before and after the exercise.

Exercise 2: Visualization Techniques

Objective: Enhance mental resilience and performance.

Description: Practice visualizing successful outcomes for various scenarios.

Duration: 10 minutes daily.

Instructions: Close your eyes and vividly imagine yourself overcoming challenges and achieving goals. Engage all your senses in the visualization process.

Physical Resilience Drills

Exercise 1: High-Intensity Interval Training (HIIT)

Objective: Improve physical and mental resilience.

Description: Perform short bursts of high-intensity exercises followed by brief rest periods.

Duration: 20-30 minutes.

Instructions: Include exercises like sprints, burpees, and jump squats.

Push yourself to your limits and focus on maintaining form.

Exercise 2: Yoga and Flexibility

Objective: Enhance physical resilience and mental calm.

Description: Practice yoga poses that improve flexibility and strength.

Duration: 30 minutes daily.

Instructions: Follow a guided yoga routine focusing on deep breathing and mindfulness. Reflect on how the practice affects your mental state.

Emotional Resilience Drills

Exercise 1: Journaling

Objective: Build emotional resilience through self-reflection.

Description: Write about your thoughts, feelings, and experiences daily.

Duration: 15-20 minutes.

Instructions: Focus on expressing your emotions honestly and identifying patterns in your reactions. Reflect on how you can better manage your emotions.

Exercise 2: Gratitude Practice

Objective: Foster a positive mindset and emotional resilience.

Description: Write down three things you are grateful for each day.

Duration: 5 minutes daily.

Instructions: Be specific about what you are grateful for and why. Reflect on how this practice shifts your emotional state over time.

Performance Enhancement Drills

<u>Exercise 1: Time Blocking</u>

Objective: Improve productivity and focus.

Description: Schedule specific blocks of time for different tasks throughout the day.

Duration: Plan for the entire day.

Instructions: Prioritize tasks based on importance and urgency. Stick to your schedule and minimize distractions during each time block.

<u>Exercise 2: Pomodoro Technique</u>

Objective: Enhance concentration and efficiency.

Description: Work in focused intervals (usually 25 minutes) followed by short breaks.

Duration: 25 minutes work, 5 minutes break.

Instructions: Use a timer to keep track of intervals. During breaks, engage in activities that help you relax and recharge.

Recovery and Regeneration Drills

<u>Exercise 1: Progressive Muscle Relaxation (PMR)</u>

Objective: Reduce stress and promote physical recovery.

Description: Tense and then relax different muscle groups.

Duration: 10-15 minutes.

Instructions: Start from your toes and work your way up to your head, tensing each muscle group for 5 seconds before releasing. Focus on the sensation of relaxation.

<u>Exercise 2: Sleep Optimization</u>

Objective: Enhance recovery through quality sleep.

Description: Develop a consistent sleep routine and create an optimal sleep environment.

Duration: 7-9 hours of sleep per night.

Instructions: Go to bed and wake up at the same time every day. Create a dark, quiet, and cool sleep environment. Avoid screens and stimulating activities before bedtime.

These exercises are designed to build resilience and enhance performance by targeting various aspects of mental, physical, and emotional well-being. Integrate them into your daily routine and observe the positive in your overall well-being.

Checklist for Continuous Improvement

Morning Routine

Wake up at a consistent time.

Hydrate with a glass of water.

Engage in a brief physical activity (e.g., stretching or a short walk).

Practice 5 minutes of mindfulness or meditation.

Review daily goals and prioritize tasks.

Work and Productivity

Implement time blocking for key tasks.

Use the Pomodoro Technique to maintain focus.

Take regular breaks to prevent burnout.

Review and adjust the to-do list as needed.

Avoid multitasking to enhance productivity.

Physical Health

Engage in at least 30 minutes of physical exercise.

Follow a balanced diet with nutritious meals.

Stay hydrated throughout the day.

Practice progressive muscle relaxation (PMR) in the evening.

Mental and Emotional Well-being

Journal your thoughts and experiences.

Practice gratitude by listing three things you're thankful for.

Spend quality time with family or friends.

Engage in a relaxing activity before bed (e.g., reading or listening to music).

Evening Routine

Reflect on the day's achievements and areas for improvement.

Plan tasks and goals for the next day.

Create a conducive sleep environment (dark, quiet, cool).

Aim for 7-9 hours of quality sleep.

Weekly Checklist

At the end of each week, take time to assess your progress towards your goals. Reflect on what you have accomplished and identify any challenges you faced. This assessment allows you to adjust your strategies and set new targets for the upcoming week. By regularly reviewing your goals, you can stay focused and ensure continuous improvement in your personal and professional life. Continuous learning is key to staying competitive and innovative. Dedicate time each week to develop new skills or expand your knowledge. This can involve reading a book or article related to your field or personal interests, attending a workshop, or participating in a webinar. Engaging in regular learning activities helps you stay current and open to new ideas, fostering long-term growth. Maintaining your health requires a balanced approach to physical activity and psychical well-being. Vary your exercise routine to include different activities, ensuring all aspects of fitness are addressed. In addition to physical workouts, practice mindfulness or meditation for a longer session once a week. This can help you manage stress and maintain inner clarity. Plan a day with lighter activities or complete rest to rejuvenate both your body and mind, preventing burnout and enhancing overall performance. Strong social connections provide support and motivation. Make an effort each week to connect with mentors or coaches who can offer guidance and insights. Engage in meaningful conversations with family or friends to strengthen your relationships. Participating in community or networking events can also expand your social circle and open up new opportunities for collaboration and support. By incorporating these weekly practices, you can ensure steady progress towards your goals, continuous learning, and a balanced approach to health and well-being. These practices are designed to help you stay focused, motivated, and resilient, fostering long-term success and personal growth.

Monthly Checklist

At the end of each week, take time to assess your progress towards your goals. Reflect on what you have accomplished and identify any challenges you faced. This assessment allows you to adjust your plans and set new targets for the upcoming week. By regularly reviewing your goals, you can stay focused and ensure continuous improvement in your personal and professional life. Continuous learning is key to staying competitive and innovative. Dedicate time each week to develop new skills or expand your knowledge. This can involve reading a book or article related to your field or personal interests, attending a workshop, or participating in a webinar. Vary your exercise routine to include different activities, ensuring all aspects of fitness are addressed. In addition to physical workouts, practice mindfulness or meditation for a longer session once a week. This can help you manage stress and maintain inner clarity. Plan a day with lighter activities or complete rest to rejuvenate both your body and mind, preventing burnout and enhancing overall performance. Strong social connections provide support and motivation. Make an effort each week to connect with mentors or coaches who can offer guidance and insights. Engage in meaningful conversations with family or friends to strengthen your relationships. Participating in community or networking events can also expand your social circle and open up new opportunities for collaboration and support. By incorporating these weekly practices, you can ensure steady progress towards your goals, continuous learning, and a balanced approach to health and well-being. These practices are designed to help you stay focused, motivated, and resilient, fostering long-term success and personal growth.

Annual Checklist

Conduct a comprehensive review of your progress towards yearly goals. Assess significant achievements and identify areas where improvement is needed. Reflect on the ones that worked well and those that didn't, making necessary adjustments for the upcoming year. Set new major goals that align with your long-term vision and aspirations, ensuring continuous progress and growth. Evaluate your career progress over the past year and set new professional goals. Consider opportunities for further education or certification to enhance your skills and stay competitive in your field. Update your resume and professional portfolio with new accomplishments and experiences. Plan for potential career transitions or advancements, and seek out new challenges that align with your professional ambitions. Reflect on your personal growth and relationships throughout the year. Set new personal development goals that align with your values and aspirations. Plan significant life events or milestones, such as travel, learning a new hobby, or achieving a personal milestone. Focus on building habits that support your personal growth and well-being. Schedule comprehensive health and wellness check-ups to monitor your physical and mental health. Review and adjust your long-term health and fitness plans to ensure they meet your evolving needs and goals. Plan a major vacation or a personal retreat to recharge and rejuvenate, helping to maintain a balanced approach to health and wellness throughout the year. Review your annual financial statements and adjust your financial plan accordingly. Reflect on your financial goals and progress, making necessary adjustments to your budget and savings strategies. Plan for major expenses or investments in the upcoming year, such as buying a home, starting a business, or saving for retirement. Set new financial goals and savings targets to ensure long-term financial stability and growth. Take time to reflect on the past year's achievements and challenges, gaining insights into your progress and areas for improvement. Plan significant projects or activities for the upcoming year to stay organized and focused. Celebrate your accomplishments and reward yourself for the hard work and dedication you have shown. Use this reflection to fuel your motivation and set a clear vision for the year ahead. By integrating these annual practices, you can maintain a clear trajectory towards your long-term goals, ensure continuous professional and personal development, and uphold a balanced approach to health and well-being. Regularly revisiting these practices will help you stay focused, motivated, and prepared for future challenges, fostering long-term success and personal growth.

This checklist is designed to foster continuous improvement in various aspects of life, ensuring balanced progress and well-being. Regularly revisiting these checklists can help maintain focus and drive long-term success.

Templates for Performance Planning

Daily Performance Planning Template

Date: ___________

Morning Routine:

1. Wake-up time: ____________

2. Hydration: ___________ (e.g., Glass of water)

3. Physical Activity: ___________ (e.g., Stretching, short walk)

4. Mindfulness/Meditation: ___________ minutes

5. Daily Goals Review:

   - Goal 1: ___________

   - Goal 2: ___________

   - Goal 3: ___________

Work and Productivity:

1. Time Blocking Schedule:

   - Task 1: ___________ (Start Time: _____, End Time: _____)

   - Task 2: ___________ (Start Time: _____, End Time: _____)

   - Task 3: ___________ (Start Time: _____, End Time: _____)

2. Pomodoro Sessions:

   - Session 1: ___________ (Start Time: _____, End Time: _____)

   - Session 2: ___________ (Start Time: _____, End Time: _____)

   - Session 3: ___________ (Start Time: _____, End Time: _____)

3. Breaks:

   - Break 1: ______ minutes (Start Time: _____, End Time: _____)

   - Break 2: ______ minutes (Start Time: _____, End Time: _____)

   - Break 3: ______ minutes (Start Time: _____, End Time: _____)

Physical Health:

1. Exercise: ___________ (Type and Duration)

2. Balanced Diet Plan:

    o Breakfast: ___________

    o Lunch: ___________

    o Dinner: ___________

    o Snacks: ___________

3. Hydration: ___________ glasses of water

Mental and Emotional Well-being:

1. Journaling: ___________ minutes (Topics: ___________)

2. Gratitude Practice: List 3 things you're grateful for:

    o ____

    o ____

    o ____

3. Quality Time with Family/Friends:______ minutes(Activity:____)

Evening Routine:

1. Reflection on Daily Achievements: ___________

2. Plan for Next Day: ___________ (Tasks/Goals)

3. Sleep Routine:

    o Bedtime: ___________

    o Wake-up Time: ___________

4. Relaxing Activity: ___________ (e.g., Reading, listening to music)

Weekly Performance Planning Template

Week: ___________

Goal Review:

1. Weekly Goals Assessment:

   o   Goal 1: ___________ (Progress: ___________)

   o   Goal 2: ___________ (Progress: ___________)

   o   Goal 3: ___________ (Progress: ___________)

2. Adjustments for Next Week:

   o   Adjustment 1: ___________

   o   Adjustment 2: ___________

   o   Adjustment 3: ___________

Learning and Development:

1. Skill/Knowledge Development:

   o   Activity 1: ___________ (e.g., Read a book/article)

   o   Activity 2: ___________ (e.g., Attend a workshop/webinar)

2. Time Dedicated: ___________ minutes/hours

Physical and Mental Health:

1. Vary Exercise Routine:

   o   Exercise 1: ___________ (Type and Duration)

   o   Exercise 2: ___________ (Type and Duration)

2. Mindfulness/Meditation Session: ___________ minutes

3. Rest/Light Activity Day: ___________ (Activity: ___________)

Social Connections:

1. Mentor/Coach Interaction:

    o Person: ___________

    o Date: ___________

    o Topics: ___________

2. Family/Friends Quality Time:

    o Activity: ___________

    o Duration: ___________

3. Community/Networking Event:

    o Event: ___________

    o Date: ___________

Monthly Performance Planning Template

Month: __________

Long-term Goal Assessment:

1. Monthly Goals Review:

    o Goal 1: __________ (Progress: __________)

    o Goal 2: __________ (Progress: __________)

    o Goal 3: __________ (Progress: __________)

2. Adjustments for Next Month:

    o Adjustment 1: __________

    o Adjustment 2: __________

    o Adjustment 3: __________

Professional Development:

1. Resume/Portfolio Update:

    o New Skills/Experiences: __________

2. Networking Activities:

    o Activity 1: __________ (Event/Platform: __________)

    o Activity 2: __________ (Event/Platform: __________)

3. Further Education/Skill Enhancement:

    o Course/Certification: __________

    o Duration: __________

Health and Wellness:

1. Health Check-up/Consultation:
   - Appointment Date: ___________
   - Key Points: ___________
2. Diet and Exercise Review:
   - Changes Needed: ___________
3. Planned Vacation/Mini-Retreat:
   - Destination: ___________
   - Dates: ___________

Social Connections:

1. Mentor/Coach Interaction:
   - Person: ___________
   - Date: ___________
   - Key Topics: ___________
2. Family/Friends Engagement:
   - Activity: ___________
   - Duration: ___________
3. Community/Networking Event:
   - Event: ___________
   - Date: ___________

Financial Health:

1. Budget Review and Adjustment:

   o Changes Needed: __________

2. Expenses and Savings Tracking:

   o Insights: __________

3. Future Financial Goals/Investments:

   o Goal/Investment: __________

   o Plan: __________

Reflection and Planning:

1. Monthly Reflection:

   o Achievements: __________

   o Setbacks: __________

2. Plan for Next Month:

   o Significant Projects/Activities: __________

3. Celebrating Accomplishments:

   o Reward/Recognition: __________

Annual Performance Planning Template

Year: __________

Yearly Review:

1. Long-term Goals Review:

    - Goal 1: __________ (Progress: __________)

    - Goal 2: __________ (Progress: __________)

    - Goal 3: __________ (Progress: __________)

2. Strategy Adjustments:

    - Adjustment 1: __________

    - Adjustment 2: __________

    - Adjustment 3: __________

3. New Major Goals:

    - Goal 1: __________

    - Goal 2: __________

    - Goal 3: __________

Professional Growth:

1. Career Progress Evaluation:

    - Key Achievements: __________

    - Areas for Improvement: __________

2. Further Education/Certifications:

    - Course/Certification: __________

    - Plan: __________

3. Resume/Portfolio Update:

    - New Skills/Experiences: __________

Personal Development:

1. Personal Growth Reflection:
   - Key Insights: ___________
   - Areas for Improvement: ___________
2. New Personal Development Goals:
   - Goal 1: ___________
   - Goal 2: ___________
   - Goal 3: ___________
3. Significant Life Events Planning:
   - Event/Milestone: ___________
   - Plan: ___________

Health and Wellness:

1. Comprehensive Health Check-up:
   - Appointment Date: ___________
   - Key Points: ___________
2. Health and Fitness Plan Review:
   - Changes Needed: ___________
3. Major Vacation/Personal Retreat:
   - Destination: ___________
   - Dates: ___________

Financial Planning:

1. Annual Financial Statement Review:

    o Key Insights: ___________

    o Adjustments: ___________

2. Major Expenses/Investments Planning:

    o Expense/Investment: ___________

    o Plan: ___________

New Financial Goals:

    o Goal 1: ___________

    o Goal 2: ___________

    o Goal 3: ___________

Reflection and Planning:

1. Annual Reflection:

    o Achievements: ___________

    o Challenges: ___________

    o Key Learnings: ___________

2. Planning for Next Year:

    o Major Projects/Activities: ___________

    o Strategies: ___________

3. Celebrating Accomplishments:

    o Reward/Recognition: ___________

By using these templates, you can systematically plan and track your performance, ensuring continuous improvement and balanced progress across various aspects of your life.

FAQ on Resilience and Mental Performance

1. What is resilience, and why is it important? Resilience is the ability to adapt and bounce back from adversity, trauma, or significant stress. It's a crucial trait because it enables individuals to cope with challenges, maintain mental well-being, and continue functioning effectively despite difficult circumstances. Resilience provides the foundation for enduring tough times and emerging stronger.

2. How can I develop a resilient mindset? Developing a resilient mindset involves cultivating a positive outlook, building strong relationships, setting realistic goals, embracing change, and developing problem-solving skills. It's about training your mind to see challenges as opportunities for growth rather than insurmountable obstacles. Surrounding yourself with supportive people, breaking down large goals into manageable steps, and approaching problems proactively are all essential components of this mindset.

3. What role does physical health play in resilience? Physical health plays a significant role in resilience. When your body is healthy, your mind can function more effectively. Regular exercise, a balanced diet, adequate sleep, and proper hydration are all crucial for maintaining physical health, which in turn supports resilience. A strong body provides the energy and stability needed to face challenges with a clear mind and a positive attitude.

4. How can mindfulness improve mental performance? Mindfulness improves mental performance by enhancing focus, reducing stress, and increasing emotional regulation. By staying present in the moment and observing your thoughts and feelings without judgment, you can improve your concentration, decision-making, and overall inner clarity. Regular awareness practice helps you manage stress more effectively and maintain a balanced, calm state of mind.

5. What are some effective strategies for managing stress? Effective stress management involves regular exercise, meditation practices, efficient time management, maintaining a healthy lifestyle, and seeking social support. Engaging in physical activity helps reduce stress hormones and boost your mood. Perception practices can calm your mind and reduce anxiety. Managing your time well and avoiding overcommitment are also key. Additionally, maintaining a balanced diet, getting enough sleep, and connecting with friends and family for support can significantly alleviate stress.

6. How can I improve my focus and concentration? Improving focus and concentration requires minimizing distractions, practicing the Pomodoro Technique, setting clear goals, staying organized, and regularly engaging in meditation exercises. Creating a dedicated workspace and limiting interruptions are vital steps. Using techniques like working in focused intervals followed by short breaks can help maintain concentration. Clearly defining your tasks and keeping your workspace tidy also contribute to better focus.

7. What is the role of goal setting in enhancing performance? Goal setting is essential for enhancing performance as it provides direction and motivation. By setting SMART (Specific, Measurable, Achievable, Relevant, Time-bound) goals, you can break down larger objectives into actionable steps. This approach helps track progress, maintain focus, and stay committed to personal and professional development, ultimately leading to greater achievement and satisfaction.

8. How can I stay motivated during challenging times? Staying motivated during challenging times involves setting short-term goals to achieve smaller milestones, celebrating successes, staying connected with supportive peers or mentors, focusing on the positive aspects of your situation, and regularly visualizing successful outcomes. By breaking down larger goals into more manageable parts, you can maintain momentum and motivation. Celebrating even small victories and connecting with others for encouragement can also provide a significant boost.

9. What techniques can help improve decision-making under pressure? Improving decision-making under pressure involves staying calm, gathering information, evaluating options, trusting your instincts, and seeking advice when necessary. Practicing deep breathing or mindfulness can help reduce anxiety and maintain a clear mind. Making informed decisions based on available data, considering the pros and cons of each option, and relying on your experience and intuition are also crucial. When needed, consulting with trusted colleagues or mentors can provide valuable perspectives.

10. How important is rest and recovery for maintaining resilience and performance? Rest and recovery are vital for maintaining resilience and performance. They allow your body and mind to repair and rejuvenate, preventing burnout and enhancing productivity.

Prioritizing adequate sleep, taking regular breaks, and engaging in activities that promote relaxation and well-being are essential practices. Ensuring you have time to recover helps sustain high levels of performance and resilience over the long term.

11. Can resilience be learned, or is it an innate trait? Resilience can be both innate and learned. While some individuals may have a natural predisposition towards resilience, anyone can develop and strengthen their resilience through practice and adopting specific strategies. Building resilience is a continuous process that involves learning from experiences, practicing positive thinking, and applying effective coping mechanisms. It's about making a conscious effort to develop the skills and mindset necessary to face challenges head-on.

12. What resources can help me further develop resilience and mental performance? Numerous resources can help you further develop resilience and mental performance. Books such as "The Resilience Factor" by Karen Reivich and Andrew Shatté and "Grit" by Angela Duckworth provide valuable insights and strategies. Online courses available on platforms like Coursera, Udemy, and Khan Academy offer structured learning opportunities. Workshops and seminars focused on personal development and resilience training can also be beneficial. Additionally, support groups and communities provide a space to share experiences, while apps like Headspace and Calm can guide you in mindfulness and meditation practices.

These insights into resilience and mental performance provide a foundation for understanding and developing these critical skills. By applying these procedures and utilizing available resources, you can enhance your ability to cope with challenges and maintain high levels of performance and well-being.

Bibliography

Clear, James. *Atomic Habits: An Easy & Proven Way to Build Good Habits & Break Bad Ones.* Avery, 2018.

Duckworth, Angela. *Grit: The Power of Passion and Perseverance.* Scribner, 2016.

Fogg, B.J. *Tiny Habits: The Small Changes That Change Everything.* Houghton Mifflin Harcourt, 2019.

Grant, Adam. *Think Again: The Power of Knowing What You Don't Know.* Viking, 2021.

Kaufman, Scott. *Transcend: The New Science of Self-Actualization.* TarcherPerigee, 2020.

Lerner, Harriet. *The Dance of Anger: A Woman's Guide to Changing the Patterns of Intimate Relationships.* HarperCollins, 1985.

Newport, Cal. *Deep Work: Rules for Focused Success in a Distracted World.* Grand Central Publishing, 2016.

Pink, Daniel H. *Drive: The Surprising Truth About What Motivates Us.* Riverhead Books, 2009.

Salzberg, Sharon. *Real Happiness: The Power of Meditation.* Workman Publishing Company, 2011.

Scott, Steve. *Millennial Money: How Young Investors Can Build a Fortune.* Wiley, 2016.

Steel, Piers. *The Procrastination Equation: How to Stop Putting Things Off and Start Getting Stuff Done.* Harper, 2010.

Young, Scott H. *Ultralearning: Master Hard Skills, Outsmart the Competition, and Accelerate Your Career.* HarperBusiness, 2019.

Webography

Harvard Business Review (HBR) Articles. *hbr.org* - Source for articles on resilience, performance, and decision-making.

Psychology Today. *psychologytoday.com* - A resource for articles and research on mental health, resilience, and emotional well-being.

Mind Tools. *mindtools.com* - Practical advice and tools for personal and professional development.

Verywell Mind. *verywellmind.com* - Articles and resources on mental health and wellness.

Positive Psychology. *positivepsychology.com* - Resources and research on positive psychology and resilience.

American Psychological Association (APA). *apa.org* - Research and articles on psychological resilience and performance.

TED Talks. *ted.com* - Talks on resilience, mental toughness, and performance by various experts.

Stanford University's Mind & Body Lab. *mindandbodylab.stanford.edu* - Research on the intersection of mental and physical well-being.

MIT Sloan Management Review. *sloanreview.mit.edu* - Articles on innovation, resilience, and performance in the business world.

The Greater Good Science Center at UC Berkeley. *greatergood.berkeley.edu* - Research and articles on resilience, well-being, and emotional intelligence.